# BOB MILLER'S SAT MATH FOR TH

# SAT MATH

## OTHER TITLES IN BOB MILLER'S CLUELESS SERIES

**BOB MILLER'S SAT MATH FOR THE CLUELESS**

# SAT MATH

*Second Edition*

## Robert Miller

**Mathematics Department**
**City College of New York**

**McGraw-Hill**

New York   Chicago   San Francisco
Lisbon   London   Madrid   Mexico City   Milan
New Delhi   San Juan   Seoul   Singapore
Sydney   Toronto

BOB MILLER'S SAT MATH FOR THE CLUELESS

7  8  9  10  11  12  DOC/DOC  1  5  4  3  2

ISBN 0-07-145287-7

SAT is a registered trademark of the College Entrance Examination Board, which was
not involved in the production of, and does not endorse, this product.

Product or brand names used in this book may be trade names or trademarks. Where we
believe that there may be proprietary claims to such trade names or trademarks, the
name has been used with an initial capital or it has been capitalized in the style used by
the name claimant. Regardless of the capitalization used, all such names have been
used in an editorial manner without any intent to convey endorsement of or other affili-
ation with name claimant. Neither the author nor the publisher intends to express any
judgment as to the validity or legal status of any such proprietary claims.

**Library of Congress Cataloging-in-Publication Data**

Miller, Robert
   Bob Miller's SAT math for the clueless / Bob Miller. — 2nd ed.
     p. cm.
   ISBN 0-07-145287-7 (alk. paper)
   1. Mathematics—Problems, exercises, etc. 2. Scholastic Aptitude Test—Study guides.
I. Title: SAT math for the clueless. II. Title.
   QA43.M494 2004
   510′.76—dc22

                              2004030769

*To my wife, Marlene, I dedicate this book and everything else
I ever do to you. I love you very, very much.*

# CONTENTS

# TO THE STUDENT

This book is written for you: not your teacher, not your next-door neighbor, not for anyone but you. It is written so that you might improve your math SAT score by 50 or 100 points, or maybe even a little more.

However, as much as I hate to admit it, I am not perfect. If anything is unclear, or if you would like to see a topic covered in future editions, please visit my Web site at www.mathclueless.com to post a comment. I can also be reached at bobmiller@mathclueless.com.

Now, enjoy the book and learn!!!!!

# HOW TO USE THIS BOOK

This book, if used properly, is designed for you to do great on your SAT. It is written in small bits of explanation that are followed immediately by problems. Read carefully the examples that explain each skill, and try each of the problems that are there for you to practice. Buuuut . . . beware!!! Even the best students, the first or second time through, make mistakes, lots of mistakes. This is NOT important. The only day that counts is the day you take the SAT. Next, read the solution to each problem. Make sure you understand what was done in each problem. Quality study is much more important than quantity. Speed is NOT important until you get to the actual test. You will automatically go faster when you know the material and know the tricks. Give yourself enough time before the SAT so that you can learn everything. Enjoy the practice. I love to do these kinds of questions. I hope you soon will too.

# ACKNOWLEDGMENTS

I have many people to thank.

I thank my wife Marlene, who makes life worth living, who is the wind under my wings.

I thank the rest of my family: children and in-law children Sheryl and Eric, Glenn and Wanda, grandchildren Kira, Evan, Sean, and Sarah, brother Jerry; and parents and in-law parents, Cele and Lee, Edith and Siebeth.

I thank those at McGraw-Hill: Barbara Gilson, Maureen Walker, and Adrinda Kelly.

I would like to thank former employees of McGraw-Hill: John Carleo, John Aliano, David Beckwith, Mary Loebig Giles, Pat Koch, Andrew Littell, and Meagan McGovern.

I thank Martin Levine of Market Source for introducing my books to McGraw-Hill.

I thank Daryl Davis, Bernice Rothstein, Sy Solomon, and Dr. Robert Urbanski.

As usual, the last thanks go to three terrific people: a great friend Gary Pitkofsky; another terrific friend and fellow teacher David Schwinger; and my sharer of dreams, my cousin Keith Robin Ellis.

# I WANT YOU TO IMPROVE 50 POINTS OR 100 POINTS OR MORE ON THE MATH SAT

You:   What is the math SAT?

Me:   It is a game!

You:   What is the object of the game??

Me:   What is the object of any game?

You:   To win.

Me:   Right. And what do you win?

You:   Well, what DO I win??

Me:   The college of your choice!! Let me give you an example of the game. Remember, you should do no writing with this problem, none at all.

You:   But the teacher always told me to show all the work and write everything down. I can't do it any other way. I can't. I can't! I CAN'T!!!!!!

Me:   Sure you can, but it may take a little time to learn. Remember, it is not important that you get the problem right the first or second time. The only important time is the day of the SAT.

You:   OK, OK. Llllet's sssseee the problem.

Me:   If $2x - 1 = 80$, what is $2x - 3$? No, no, no! Don't solve for x. Just look at $2x - 1$ . . . then look at $2x - 3$. . . .

You:   It looks like 2 less.

Me:   That's right!!! So the answer is . . .

You:   78!!! 78!!!!

Me:   That's terrific. $2x - 1$ to $2x - 3$ means you go down 2. $80 - 2 = 78$.

You:   I would never think of this on my own.

Me:   Maybe not now, but after you read this book, you'll be muuuuch better!! It will help you in your regular math class also. It will also make math more fun because you'll be able to work quicker with less writing.

You:   I'll bet you have to know a zillion facts to improve 50 or 100 points on the math SAT.

Me:   Oddly, this is not true. You need to know relatively few things, but you must do them the SAT way.

You:   What is the math SAT anyway?

Me:   It is a reading test, a speed test, a trick test, but not really a math test. And you really don't need to know a zillion facts.

You:   So how is this book written?

Me:   The book is divided into bite-size portions, first with instructions, then with practice problems. Then there are practice SATs at the end to see how you're doing.

You:   I understand calculators can be used on the SAT! Yay!!!

Me:   Stop cheering. If you look at the top of each math section, you see stuff you need for the test. If you need to look at these formulas, you will never, NEVER do well on this test.

The same is almost true for calculators. A calculator may (just may) give you one or two answers, but it will slow you down so much you probably won't finish all the questions in a section. Let me show you an example:

$$\frac{2}{3} \times \frac{3}{4} \times \frac{4}{5} \times \frac{5}{6} \times \frac{6}{7} \times \frac{7}{8} \times \frac{8}{9} \times \frac{9}{10} \times \frac{10}{11} \times \frac{11}{12} \times \frac{12}{13} \times \frac{13}{14}$$

If you use a calculator, it will take nearly forever. But if you remember your arithmetic and cancel. . . .

$$\frac{2}{\cancel{3}} \times \frac{\cancel{3}}{\cancel{4}} \times \frac{\cancel{4}}{\cancel{5}} \times \frac{\cancel{5}}{\cancel{6}} \times \frac{\cancel{6}}{\cancel{7}} \times \frac{\cancel{7}}{\cancel{8}} \times \frac{\cancel{8}}{\cancel{9}} \times \frac{\cancel{9}}{\cancel{10}} \times \frac{\cancel{10}}{\cancel{11}} \times \frac{\cancel{11}}{\cancel{12}} \times \frac{\cancel{12}}{\cancel{13}} \times \frac{\cancel{13}}{14} = \frac{2}{14}$$

You can do all the canceling in your head and get 2/14 = 1/7 in about 8 seconds!!!!

You:   That is really neat!! I'm ready!!! Let's get started!!!!

# SAT MATH

The SAT loves fractions but virtually never asks you to do pure computational problems—you know, the ones you need a calculator for. You must know what fractions are and how to compare them. This is how I usually begin.

Suppose I'm 6 years old. Can you please tell me what 3/7 is? Remember, I don't know division. So I can't change a fraction to a decimal. Heck, I don't even know what a decimal is.

OK, I'm a smart 6-year-old. Suppose I have a pizza pie. . . . That is right. You divide it into 7 EQUAL parts, and I get 3 pieces.

**Words and Symbols You Need:**

*Sum:* **The answer in addition**

*Difference:* **The answer in subtraction**

*Product:* **The answer in multiplication**

*Quotient:* **The answer in division**

**a > b, read a is greater than b, is the same as b < a, read b is less than a.**

**Also, negatives "reverse":**

**2 < 3    buuut    −2 > −3**

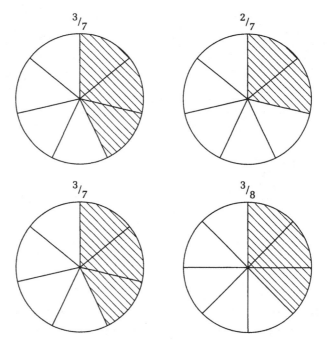

But which is bigger, 2/7 or 3/7?

3/7 is bigger: 3/7 > 2/7 because 3 equal pieces are more than 2.

But which is bigger, 3/7 or 3/8?

Again, it is 3/7 because 3 larger pieces are more than 3 smaller pieces.

For positive fractions, if the BOTTOMS are the same, the bigger the top, the BIGGER the fraction. If the TOPS are the same, the bigger the bottom, the SMALLER the fraction.

For negative fractions, the opposite is true, although the SAT rarely compares negative fractions.

Trick for **adding fractions:**

$$\frac{a}{b} - \frac{c}{d} = \frac{ad - bc}{bd}$$

**Reason:**

$$\frac{a}{b} - \frac{c}{d} = \frac{ad}{bd} - \frac{bc}{bd} = \frac{ad - bc}{bd}$$

$$\frac{3}{10} - \frac{2}{11} = \frac{33 - 20}{110}$$

To **mulllltiply fractions,** always cancel before you multiply the tops and the bottoms:

$$a \times \frac{b}{c} = \frac{ab}{c}$$

**Reason:**

$$a \times \frac{b}{c} = \frac{a}{1} \times \frac{b}{c} = \frac{ab}{c}$$

To **double a fraction,** double the top or take ½ of the bottom:

Twice 5/7 is 10/7, and twice 7/6 is 7/3 (or 14/6, which = 7/3).

Here is one the SAT loves and is frequently overlooked, comparing a positive fraction to 1. This sounds simple but is not quite that.

If you add the same positive number to a fraction less than 1, it gets bigger:

$$\frac{3}{4} < \frac{3+6}{4+6} = \frac{9}{10}$$

If you add the same positive number to a fraction bigger than 1, it gets smaller:

$$\frac{3}{2} > \frac{3+1}{2+1} = \frac{4}{3}$$

## LET'S TRY SOME PROBLEMS

The answers are explained on the next page. Do not get discouraged. Most people get most of the answers wrong the first time or two through. Reread each problem until you understand the skill. Remember, only the day of the SAT counts. By then you'll do fine.

**EXAMPLE 1—**

$$\frac{a}{b} - \frac{a}{d}$$

**EXAMPLE 2—**

Which is the smallest value?

A. $\dfrac{1/2}{1/4}$　　B. $\dfrac{1/3}{1/4}$　　C. $\dfrac{1/4}{1/5}$　　D. $\dfrac{1/3}{1/3}$

E. $\dfrac{1/4}{1/3}$

**EXAMPLE 3—**

Which is the largest value?

A. $\dfrac{1}{6}$　　B. $\dfrac{1}{60}$　　C. $\dfrac{1}{.06}$

D. $\dfrac{1}{600}$　　E. $\left(\dfrac{1}{.06}\right)^2$

**EXAMPLE 4—**

Which is the largest value?

A. $\dfrac{a}{b}$　　B. $\dfrac{a-1}{b-1}$　　C. $\dfrac{a+1}{b+1}$

D. $\dfrac{a+100}{b+100}$　　　　E.　Can't tell.

**EXAMPLE 5—**

$\dfrac{1}{1+\dfrac{1}{b}} = p$　　Which expression is 2p?

A. $\dfrac{2}{2+\dfrac{2}{b}}$　　B. $\dfrac{2}{2+\dfrac{1}{b}}$　　C. $\dfrac{1}{\dfrac{1}{2}+\dfrac{1}{2b}}$

D. $\dfrac{1}{1+\dfrac{2}{b}}$　　E. $\dfrac{1}{2+\dfrac{1}{2b}}$

**EXAMPLE 6—**

If x ranges from .0002 to .02 and y goes from .2 to 20, what is the maximum value of x/y?

# SOLUTIONS

**EXAMPLE 1—**

This should be simple:

$$\frac{ad - ab}{bd}$$

**EXAMPLE 2—**

You don't need to do arithmetic on this fraction. Really you don't! A fraction is bigger than 1 if the top is bigger than the bottom: A, B, and C. D equals 1. The answer is E since it is the only fraction where the bottom is bigger than the top, and the value of the fraction is less than 1.

**EXAMPLE 3—**

Eliminate A, B, and D since they are less than 1. D and E are both bigger than 1. E is the square of D. When you square a number bigger than 1, it is bigger.  The answer is E, E, E.

**EXAMPLE 4—**

Tough. The answer is E, you can't tell.

1.  If a = b (the problem doesn't say it can't), then

    $$\frac{a}{b} = \frac{a+1}{b+1} \qquad \frac{5}{5} = \frac{6}{6}$$

2.  If a < b, then $\qquad \dfrac{a}{b} < \dfrac{a+1}{b+1} \qquad \dfrac{2}{3} < \dfrac{3}{4}$

3.  If a > b, then $\qquad \dfrac{a}{b} > \dfrac{a+1}{b+1} \qquad \dfrac{5}{4} > \dfrac{6}{5}$

and we didn't even look at negative fractions!!!!

**EXAMPLE 5—**

Tuff. A equals p because we doubled both the top and bottom. B, D, and E are mixes. The answer is C because we took half of the bottom.

**EXAMPLE 6—**

Any positive fraction is largest with the biggest top and the smallest bottom. .02/.2 = 1/10 = .1 because the question was really a multiple-choice one, but I wanted you to answer it without the choices since there are non-multiple-choice answers.

If you need more help with fractions and decimals, see *Algebra for the Clueless*.

## CHAPTER 2

# CAN WE COMPARE? (YES!) THE POWERS THAT BE

Which is bigger $a^2$ or a? The answer is, we can't tell, but it is important to know why:

If a > 1, then $a^2$ > a:     $3^2$ > 3.

If a = 1, then $1^2$ = 1.

If 0 < a < 1, then $a^2$ < a since $(½)^2$ = ¼ < ½.

I'll bet some of you didn't know that when you square a number, sometimes it gets smaller. This is how the SAT gets you, but not now!!!

If a = 0, $a^2$ = a since $0^2$ = 0.

If a < 0 (negative), $a^2$ is bigger because squaring a number makes it positive, which is always bigger than a negative:

$(-4)^2$ > −4 since 16 > −4.

**NOTE**

If we compared $a^3$ and $a^2$, everything would be the same exceptttt if $a < 0$, then $a^2 > a^3$ because a positive is > a negative: $(-4)^2 > (-4)^3$, $16 > -64$.

There are a zillion problems about this on the SAT (slight exaggeration). Let's do a few.

## PROBLEMS

**EXAMPLE 1**

$0 < x < 1$.     Which is arranged smallest to largest?

A. $x, x^2, x^3$     B. $x, x^3, x^2$     C. $x^3, x^2, x$
D. $x^3, x, x^2$     E. $x^2, x, x^3$

**EXAMPLE 2**

$-1 < x < 0$.     Which is arranged smallest to largest?

A. $x, x^2, x^3$     B. $x, x^3, x^2$     C. $x^3, x^2, x$
D. $x^3, x, x^2$     E. $x^2, x, x^3$

**EXAMPLE 3**

$-1 \le x \le 4$.     Where is $x^2$ located?

A. $-1 \le x^2 \le 4$     B. $0 \le x^2 \le 16$     C. $1 \le x^2 \le 4$
D. $1 \le x^2 \le 8$     E. $1 \le x^2 \le 16$

**EXAMPLE 4**

x and y are positive integers. Which is the biggest?

A. $x + y$     B. $x^2 + y^2$     C. $x + y + 1$
D. $x^2 + y^2 + 1$     E. $(x + y)^2$

**EXAMPLE 5—**

a, b, and c are integers all between 2 and 8. Which average (mean) is the largest?

A. $a + b + c$     B. $a + b + c + 2$     C. $a^2 + b^2 + c^2$
D. $a^2 + b^2 + 4$     E. Can't tell.

**EXAMPLE 6—**

Which is the biggest?

A. $.5m + .7p$     B. $.7m + .5p$     C. $.5(m + p)$
D. $.6(m + p)$     E. Can't tell.

**EXAMPLE 7—**

$-2 < x < -1$.     Which is the smallest?

A. $x$     B. $-x$     C. $1/x$     D. $-1/x$     E. $1/x^2$

# SOLUTIONS

**EXAMPLE 1—**

Suppose $x = 1/2$; $x^2 = 1/4$; $x^3 = 1/8$. The answer is C.

**EXAMPLE 2—**

Suppose $x = -1/2$; $x^2 = 1/4$; $x^3 = -1/8$. The answer is B. Remember, $-1/2 < -1/8$.

**EXAMPLE 3—**

Verrry tricky. The answer is B. If you square every number from $-1$ through 4 inclusive, you have to remember you also square 0. Also, 4 squared is 16!

**EXAMPLE 4—**

The answer is E because $(x + y)^2 = x^2 + 2xy + y^2 > x^2 + y^2 + 1$.

**EXAMPLE 5—**

The answer is C. If the numbers are between 2 and 8, they can't equal 2 or 8.

a, b, and c must all be at least 3. Sooo, C must be the largest.

**EXAMPLE 6—**

The answer is E. We can't tell since the letters could be positive, negative, or zero.

**EXAMPLE 7—**

Eliminate B, D, and E because they are all positive.

If $x = -3/2$, then $1/x = -2/3$, which is bigger than $-3/2$. The answer is A.

## CHAPTER 3

# ROOTS, LIKE SQUARE, MAN

The SAT also adores square roots. The SAT never asks you to calculate the square root of 123456789.234, especially with calculators, but you should know the following:

1. $\sqrt{2} = 1.4$ (approx), and $\sqrt{3} = 1.7$ (also approx).

2. $\sqrt{0} = 0$, $\sqrt{1} = 1$, $\sqrt{4} = 2$, $\sqrt{9} = 3$, $\sqrt{16} = 4$, $\sqrt{25} = 5$, $\sqrt{36} = 6$, $\sqrt{49} = 7$, $\sqrt{64} = 8$, $\sqrt{81} = 9$, $\sqrt{100} = 10$. Even with calculators, it is good to know these.

3. $\sqrt{\dfrac{4}{9}} = \dfrac{\sqrt{4}}{\sqrt{9}} = \dfrac{2}{3}$.

4. Simplify $\sqrt{72}$: $\sqrt{(2)(2)(2)(3)(3)} = (3)(2)\sqrt{2} = 6\sqrt{2}$. Also . . . $10\sqrt{72} = 10(6)\sqrt{2} = 60\sqrt{2}$.

5. $2\sqrt{3} + 4\sqrt{5} + 6\sqrt{3} + 7\sqrt{5} = 8\sqrt{3} + 11\sqrt{5}$.

6. Rationalize the denominator:

$$\frac{8}{\sqrt{6}} = \frac{8\sqrt{6}}{\sqrt{6}\sqrt{6}} = \frac{8\sqrt{6}}{6} = \frac{4\sqrt{6}}{3}$$

7. $(a\sqrt{b})(c\sqrt{d}) = ac\sqrt{bd}$.

**REASON: 8 is true because if you square $\sqrt{x+y}$, you get $x+y$. If you square $\sqrt{x} + \sqrt{y}$, you get $x + y + a$ middle term.**

8. If x, y are positive, then $\sqrt{x} + \sqrt{y} > \sqrt{x+y}$.

And just as we compared a and $a^2$, we want to compare a and $\sqrt{a}$.

If $a > 1$, then $a > \sqrt{a}$ since $4 > \sqrt{4}$.

If $a = 1$, then $a = \sqrt{a}$ since $1 = \sqrt{1}$.

**This is a demonstration like p7. I'll bet some of you didn't know that sometimes, when you take a square root, the number becomes bigger.**

If $0 < a < 1$, then $\sqrt{a} > a$ !!!!    $\sqrt{\frac{1}{4}} = \frac{1}{2} > \frac{1}{4}$.

If $a = 0$, then $\sqrt{0} = 0$, and $a = \sqrt{a}$.

a can't be negative because $\sqrt{a}$ is imaginary, a no-no for the SAT, at least up to now.

## LET'S TRY SOME PROBLEMS

### EXAMPLE 1

$(\sqrt{5} + \sqrt{7})^2 - (\sqrt{12})^2 =$

A. 0    B. $\sqrt{35}$    C. $2\sqrt{35}$
D. 35    E. 70

### EXAMPLE 2

If $0 < M < 1$, which of the following are true?

I. $M > M^3$

II. $M^2 > 1/M^2$

III. $M > 1/\sqrt{M}$

A. I only    B. II only    C. I and II    D. III only
E. I and III

### EXAMPLE 3

$(\sqrt{32} + \sqrt{18})^2$

**EXAMPLE 4—**

$(1/4)^2 - \sqrt{1/4} = x$

A.  $-2 < x < -1$     B.  $-1 < x < 0$     C.  $0 < x < 1$
D.  $1 < x < 2$          E.  $x = 0$

## SOLUTIONS

**EXAMPLE 1—**

F.O.I.L.ing we get $5 + 2\sqrt{35} + 7 - 12 = 2\sqrt{35}$,
which is C. (F.O.I.L. = F = First, O = Outer, I = Inner,
L = Last.)

**EXAMPLE 2—**

There is usually more than one of these questions
on the SAT. So, we will do this one question in great
detail.

I is true because we know cubing a number between
0 and 1 makes it smaller (squaring also does this).

II is false. M is less than 1; $M^2$ is less than 1; $1/M^2$ is
bigger than 1.

III is false. M is less than 1; so is $\sqrt{M}$; but $\dfrac{1}{\sqrt{M}}$ is
bigger than 1.

The answer is A. This problem is important and
should be gone over.

**EXAMPLE 3—**

$\sqrt{32} = \sqrt{(2)\,(2)\,(2)\,(2)\,(2)} = 4\sqrt{2}$.

$\sqrt{18} = \sqrt{(2)\,(3)\,(3)} = 3\sqrt{2}$.

$4\sqrt{2} + 3\sqrt{2} = 7\sqrt{2}$.

$(7\sqrt{2})^2 = (7\sqrt{2})(7\sqrt{2}) = 49\sqrt{4} = 49(2) = 98$.

**EXAMPLE 4—**

1/16 − 1/2 < 0 and bigger than −1. The answer is B. Try to do this by approximation.

## CHAPTER 4

# AVERAGES

Let's try an easy topic for a change. Most students seem to like averages. Going over past SATs, I was amazed to see how many times averages occurred. The average (arithmetic mean) is the way you are graded.

## EXAMPLE 1—

Find the average (arithmetic mean) of 45, 35, 20, and 32.

$45 + 35 + 20 + 32 = 132$. $132/4$ (numbers) $= 33$, the mean

However, the SAT would NEVER ask the question this way, never!!! It would be something like this: Sandy received 76 and 89 on two tests. What must be the third test score for Sandy to have an 80 average?

### METHOD 1
80 average on three tests means $3 \times 80 = 240$ points. So far, Sandy has $76 + 89 = 165$ points. Sandy needs $240 - 165 = 75$ points.

### METHOD 2
80 average. 76 is −4 points; 80 is +9 points. So far +5 points. Needed is $80 - 5 = 75$ points since $+5 - 5 = 0$.

NOTE: The SAT always says *arithmetic mean* because there are two other words that mean "average":

*Median:* The middle number
*Mode:* The most common

We arrange the following nine numbers in order:

**2, 3, 3, 3, 7, 12, 14, 15, 19**

The median, the middle grade, is the fifth of the nine numbers, or 7.

We arrange the following ten numbers in order:

2, 3, 3, 3, 4, 7, 12, 14, 15, 19

The median, the middle grade, is the mean of the middle two numbers, the mean of the fifth and sixth $(4 + 7)/2 = 5.5$, the median.

In each case the mode, the most common, is 3.

Of the three words meaning average, the most accurate of a pretty large or large group is the MEDIAN.

I like method 2; most students like method 1. Choose the one you like.

## LET'S TRY SOME PROBLEMS

### EXAMPLE 2—

$6x + 6y = 48$. Find the average (arithmetic mean) of x and y.

### EXAMPLE 3—

In a certain city, the arithmetic mean of high readings for 4 days was 63°F. If the high readings were 62°F, 56°F, and 68°F for the first 3 days, what was the temperature the fourth day?

### EXAMPLE 4—

On a certain test, a class with 10 students has an average (arithmetic mean) of 70, and a class of 15 has an average of 90. What is the average of the 25 students?

### EXAMPLE 5—

On a certain test, the sophs had an 82 average and the juniors a 92 average.

    A.  The average is less than 87.
    B.  The average is more than 87.
    C.  The average is 87.
    D.  You can't tell what the average is.
    E.  The average is below 82 or above 92.

## SOLUTIONS

### EXAMPLE 2—

The mean of x and y is $(x + y)/2$.

$6x + 6y = 48$

Soooo $x + y = 8$     (divide by 6)

Aaaand     $\dfrac{x + y}{2} = 4$     (divide by 2)

## EXAMPLE 3—

**METHOD I**
$63 \times 4 = 252°$. $62 + 56 + 68 = 186°$. $252 - 186 = 66°F$.

**NOTICE**
186° total makes no sense, but who cares.

**METHOD 2**
Average 63°F.

62°F is −1°.

56°F is −7°.

68°F is +5°.     So far, −3° (−1 − 7 + 5 = −3).

Soo, the fourth day is $63 + 3 = 66°F$.

**NOTICE**

*It wouldn't make a difference if it were Celsius.*

## EXAMPLE 4—

The average is NOT NOT NOT 80 because the groups are not equal:

$$10(70) = \phantom{0}700 \text{ points}$$

$$15(90) = 1350 \text{ points}$$

Totals:   25       2050 points

Average:     $\dfrac{2050}{25} \times \dfrac{4}{4} = \dfrac{8200}{100} = 82$ average

**NOTICE**
You never divide by 25. You multiply by 4 and divide by 100 because 25 is 100/4, and both multiplying by 4 and dividing by 100 is way easier than dividing by 25.

**EXAMPLE 5—**

For exactly the same reason as in Example 4, the answer is D, you can't tell.

If the groups were equal size, the average would be 87.

More sophs? The average would be less than 87.

More juniors? The average would be more than 87.

## CHAPTER 5

# A LITTLE NUMBER THEORY: ODDS, EVENS, PRIMES

Another topic is number theory. No, no, no!! Not high-level stuff. I think this is the fun stuff. You need to know (if you don't already know) the following:

*Integers*: −5, −4, −3, −2, −1, 0, 1, 2, 3, 4, 5, . . .

*Positive integers*: 1, 2, 3, 4, 5, . . .

*Evens*: −6, −4, −2, 0, 2, 4, 6, . . . (remember 0 and negs)

*Odds*: −7, −5, −3, −1, 1, 3, 5, 7, . . .

*Multiples of 3*: −9, −6, −3, 0, 3, 6, 9, . . . , etc.

YOU MUST KNOW THESE *WELL*. If you do not know these, put in integers and convince yourself that:

Even + even = even     Even + odd = odd
Odd + odd = even

Even × even = even     Even × odd = even
Odd × odd = odd

If n is an integer, . . .

n + 1 is the next consecutive integer; n + 2 is the one after that, and so on.

**WARNINGS\*\*\*WARNINGS**

If the problem does NOT say "integers," then it can be any real number: fraction, irrational, any real number.

*Specifically:* a > 0 (a positive) can mean any decimal number, rational or irrational.

The sum of three consecutive integers is $n + n + 1 + n + 2 = 3n + 3$.

If n is an even integer, . . . $n + 2$ is the next, $n + 4$ is the next ($n - 2$ is the even number before n).

If n is an odd integer, . . . $n + 2$ is the next!!!! (5 is odd, $5 + 2 = 7$ is the next consecutive odd, just like the evens), the next consecutive odd is $n + 4$.

**Squaring**

If n is odd, $n^2$ is odd; aaannnd if $n^2$ is odd and n is an integer, n is odd. $3^2 = 9$ and backward.

If n is even, $n^2$ is even; aannd if $n^2$ is even and n is an integer, n is even. $6^2 = 36$ and backward.

**Factors** (also called *divisors*) are integers that "go into" a number with no remainder. We'll only look at positive ones:

Factors of 30: 1, 2, 3, 5, 6, 10, 15, 30

**Primes** are positive integers with exactly two distinct factors: itself and 1:

Prime factors of 30: 2, 3, 5

It might be nice to know the first eight: 2, 3, 5, 7, 11, 13, 17, and 19.

**NOTICE**

2 is the only even prime.

**NOTICE**

1 is <u>not</u> a prime. It has only one distinct factor, namely, 1!!!!

I love problems like the ones on this page. So does the SAT. Let's do a bunch!!!!

## PROBLEMS

**EXAMPLE 1—**

n is an integer. Which is never even?

A. 2n     B. 2n + 1     C. 3n + 2     D. 2(n − 1)
E. $2(n + 1)^3$

**EXAMPLE 2—**

The sum of two consecutive positive integers is never divisible by

A. 2     B. 3     C. 5     D. 9     E. 799

**EXAMPLE 3—**

m is odd and n is even. Which could be even?

A. m + n     B. m − n     C. m/2 + n     D. m + n/2
E. m/2 + n/2

**EXAMPLE 4—**

If the arithmetic mean (average) of 10 consecutive integers is 15½, arranged in increasing order, what is the mean of the first 5?

**EXAMPLE 5—**

$$\frac{(M - 2)(M - 4)(M - 6)(M - 20) - 1}{2}$$ is an integer if M = ?

**EXAMPLE 6—**

If q is odd, which is even?

A. q/2     B. q + 2     C. 2q + 1     D. $q^3$     E. q(q + 1)

**EXAMPLE 7—**

Which answer shows that not all odds are primes?

A. 3     B. 5     C. 7     D. 13     E. 21

**EXAMPLE 8—**

T is the set of multiples of 3. T = {. . . −9, −6, −3, 0, 3, 6, 9, . . . }. If c and d are in set T, which of the following is NOT in T?

A. cd      B. c + d      C. c − d      D. −c − d      E. c/d
F. $c^2 - d$

**EXAMPLE 9—**

If q is a whole number and q is a prime, and if 20q is divisible by 6, then q could be

A. 2      B. 3      C. 4      D. 5      E. 6

**EXAMPLE 10—**

If two odd integers are primes, which of the following is true?

   A.  Their product is an odd integer.

   B.  Their sum is prime.

   C.  Their sum is an odd integer.

   D.  Their product is prime.

   E.  The sum of their squares is prime.

   F.  Their product added to 1 is prime.

   G.  The sum of their cubes is prime.

**EXAMPLE 11—**

y is an even integer. Which is true?

   A.  Distinct prime factors of y.
   B.  Distinct prime factors of 2y.
   C.  Distinct prime factors of 4y.
   D.  Distinct prime factors of 16y.
   E.  It's a trick! They're all true!

**EXAMPLE 12—**

The sum of the first m positive integers is y. In terms of m and y, which of the following is the sum of the next m positive integers?

A. my     B. m + y     C. $m^2$ + y     D. m + $y^2$
E. 2m + y     F. m + 2y

# NOW FOR THE ANSWERS . . .

**EXAMPLE 1—**

C can be either odd or even (try n = 1 and n = 2). E, D, and A are always even because they are multiples of 2. If 2n is always even, 2n + 1 is always odd.  The answer is B.

**EXAMPLE 2—**

The sum of two consecutive integers is always odd (odd + even is odd) and is never divisible by 2. The answer is A. (A little tricky, but no hard choices to throw you off.)

**EXAMPLE 3—**

m/2 is a fraction, so C and E are no good! A and B are always odd. The answer is D. (If m = 7 and n = 22, for example.)

**EXAMPLE 4—**

15½ is the middle of 10 integers (consecutive type). Therefore, there are 5 less and 5 larger. 5 less must be 15, 14, 13, 12, 11. The average of an odd number is the middle: 13.

**EXAMPLE 5—**

This is very tough. If M is an even integer, (M − 2) × (M − 4)(M − 6)(M − 20), this product will always be even. Even −1 is odd, divided by 2 is a fraction, always. If M is odd, the product of (M − 2)(M − 4)(M − 6)(M − 20) is odd; any odd integer minus 1 is an even integer; any even integer divided by 2 is always an integer. The answer is any and all odd integers.

### EXAMPLE 6—

$q/2$ is a fraction; $q + 2$ = next consecutive odd; $2q + 1$ is always odd; $q^3$ like $q^2$ is odd. The answer is E. If q is odd, then $q + 1$ is even. The product of an odd and even is always even.

### EXAMPLE 7—

Easy one, E. 7(3) = 21.

### EXAMPLE 8—

I know, I know, the SAT has only five choices, but this is a learning process. Take c = 6 and d = 9. You will find only E is not a multiple of 3. This is true for even numbers or multiples of anything.

### EXAMPLE 9—

A, B, and D are primes. If q = B or E, 20q is divisible by 6. Only B fits both categories.

### EXAMPLE 10—

Again, the SAT doesn't have seven choices. If you take 3 and 5, only A is OK. Actually, try all of them to see what happens. Remember, this is only practice.

### EXAMPLE 11—

All are true. The SAT would not ask a question like this but I included it as a learning problem. For example:

The factors of y 5 6 are 1, 2, 3, and 6. Prime factors are 2 and 3.

The factors of 2y = 12 are 1, 2, 3, 4, 6, and 12. Prime factors are 2 and 3.

The factors of 4y = 24 are 1, 2, 3, 4, 6, 8, 12, and 24. Prime factors are 2 and 3.

The factors of 16y = 96 are 1, 2, 3, 4, 6, 8, 12, 16, 24, 32, 48, and 96, buuut the prime factors are 2 and 3.

If y were odd, B, C, and D would have one more prime factor, the number 2.

**EXAMPLE 12—**

This is truly a hard one, one of the few in this category. Let us say m = 6. Then y = 1 + 2 + 3 + 4 + 5 + 6. The next six would be 7 + 8 + 9 + 10 + 11 + 12. Looking at these differently, 7 + 8 + 9 + 10 + 11 + 12 = (1 + 6) + (2 + 6) + (3 + 6) + (4 + 6) + (5 + 6) + (6 + 6) = 1 + 2 + 3 + 4 + 5 + 6 + 6(6) = $y + 6^2$. In general, $y + m^2$. The answer is C.

**NOTE 1**

You should never worry about problems you can't do or that are strange. If you get all the ones correct that you know how to do, you'll do very fine!!!

**NOTE 2**

Never stay on one problem too long. Go on to the next and guess if you run out of time.

**NOTE 3**

Once you have answered a question, forget it and go on to the next question. NEVER, NEVER, NEVER change an answer unless you are 100% (not 99%) sure you are correct. The last time I took a test, I broke my own rule, and I changed a right answer to a wrong one.

## CHAPTER 6

# %S

Let's try to finish up the arithmetic. The biggest problem is usually %. Let's cut it down to size.

You should know the following equivalents, even with a calculator:

| | | |
|---|---|---|
| 1% = .01 = 1/100 | 10% = .10 = 1/10 | 20% = .20 = 1/5 |
| 25% = .25 = 1/4 | 30% = .30 = 3/10 | 40% = .40 = 2/5 |
| 50% = .50 = 1/2 | 60% = .60 = 3/5 | 70% = .70 = 7/10 |
| 75% = .75 = 3/4 | 80% = .80 = 4/5 | 90% = .90 = 9/10 |
| 100% = 1.0 = 1 | 200% = 2.0 = 2 | |

You should also know the following:

| | |
|---|---|
| $1/6 = .1\overline{6} = 16\frac{2}{3}\%$ | $1/3 = .\overline{3} = 33\frac{1}{3}\%$ |
| $2/3 = .\overline{6} = 66\frac{2}{3}\%$ | $5/6 = .8\overline{3} = 83\frac{1}{3}\%$ |
| $1/8 = .125 = 12\frac{1}{2}\%$ | $3/8 = .375 = 37\frac{1}{2}\%$ |
| $5/8 = .625 = 62\frac{1}{2}\%$ | $7/8 = .875 = 87\frac{1}{2}\%$ |

Even if you have been terrrrible with %s, I'll bet you'll get it now. It is the pyramid method. The goal is to get the pyramid in your head. It shouldn't be too hard.

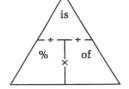

**RECALL**

$.5\overline{67} = .5676767...$

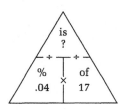

**EXAMPLE 1—**

4% of 17 is what?

$.04 \times 17 = .68$

4% = .04 goes into % box.

17 goes into the "of" box.

The chart says multiply.

That's it.

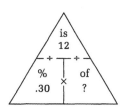

**EXAMPLE 2—**

12 is 30% of what?

$$\frac{12}{.30} = \frac{120}{3} = 40$$

12 in the "is" box.

30% = .30 in % box.

Chart says divide.

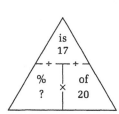

**EXAMPLE 3—**

17 is what % of 20?

$$\frac{17}{20} = 20\overline{)17.00}^{\,.85\,=\,85\%}$$

17 in the "is" box.

20 in the "of" box.

Pyramid says divide.

**REMEMBER**

**THE PYRAMID SHOULD BE IN YOUR HEAD!**

### EXAMPLE 4—

A television costs $400. If the sales tax is 8%, how much do you pay? Tax is 8% of $400. Soooo,

.08 × $400 = $32      $400 + $32 = $432

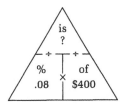

**Simple interest problems are the same:**

**Principle = $400.**
**Interest rate = 8%.**
**Interest = $400 × .08 = $32.**
**Total you have is $400 + $32 = $432.**

### EXAMPLE 5—

A $50 dress is discounted 15%. How much do you pay? Discount is on the original price. Sooo,

$50 × .15 = $7.50

You pay $50.00 − $7.50 = $42.50.

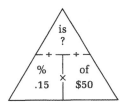

## LET'S TRY SOME

Let's do some purely arithmetic % problems.

### EXAMPLE 1—

If 15 kg of pure $H_2O$ is added to 10 kg of pure alcohol, what % by weight of the resulting solution is alcohol?

### EXAMPLE 2—

The weight of a 2000-ton truck is increased by 1%. What is the weight in tons of the increased load?

### EXAMPLE 3—

In a certain widget factory, .08% are defective. On the average, 4 will be defective. How many widgets are produced?

**EXAMPLE 4—**

In a certain country, the ratio of people over 40 to people under 40 is 3 to 2. What % of the population is under 40?

**EXAMPLE 5—**

What is 50% of 50% of 50% of 1?

## SOLUTIONS

**EXAMPLE 1—**

Alcohol is 10 kg out of a 25-kg total:

$$\frac{10}{25} = \frac{2}{5} = 40\%$$

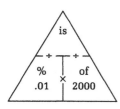

**EXAMPLE 2—**

$2000 \times .01 = 20$. $2000 + 20 = 2020$. The "tons" is there to throw you off.

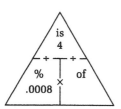

**EXAMPLE 3—**

You should read this problem as:

.08% of what (total) is 4?

.08% is not a decimal. It is a %.

.08% = .0008 (2 decimal places to the left)

$$\frac{4}{.0008} = \frac{40,000}{8} = 5000 \text{ widgets}$$

**EXAMPLE 4—**

Hopefully, you see that this is exactly Example 1 (2 out of 5 are under 40).

**EXAMPLE 5—**

This is easier done in fraction form. Repeated "of's" and % box means repeated multiplication.

½ × ½ × ½ × 1 = 1/8

% will show up later when we do charts, reading problems, ratios, and algebra. These should show you that you can do % problems!!!!!

Speaking of algebra, let's do some.

## CHAPTER 7

# SUBSTITUTE SUBSTITUTIONS

For those of you who think you have to be algebraic whizzes for the SAT and know a ton of facts, you are wrong, wrong, wrong!!! It is truly amazing how little algebra you need to do well. But you need to know how the SAT asks it. We will start with substitution (examples only) and do the rest in small pieces.

## PROBLEMS

Yes, you can do these!!

**EXAMPLE 1—**

$x = -3, y = 0 \qquad x^2y + y/x = ?$

**EXAMPLE 2—**

$(x + 4)^2 = (x - 4)^2 \qquad x =$

A. 0     B. 2     C. 4     D. 8     E. 12

**EXAMPLE 3—**

$x, y$ are positive integers, and $x > y$ and $x^2 + y^2 = 13$.
$x - y =$

A. 1     B. 2     C. 3     D. 5     E. 7

**NOTE: You must know the difference between**

$$-3^2, \quad (-3)^2, \quad -(-3)^2$$
$$-3^2 = -3(3) = -9$$
**(One minus sign = −.)**

$$(-3)^2 = (-3)(-3) = +9$$
**(Two minus signs = +.)**

$$-(-3)^2 = -(-3)(-3) = -9$$
**(Three minus signs = −.)**

**EXAMPLE 4—**

$5x = -3$      $(5x - 2)^2 =$

**EXAMPLE 5—**

If x is an integer and $2x < 24 < 3x$, then x could be _____?

**EXAMPLE 6—**

Of the following values for M, $(-1/4)^M$ will have the greatest value if M =

A. 2      B. 3      C. 4      D. 5      E. 10

**EXAMPLE 7—**

If $a = 2$ and $b = 4$, which of the following is NOT equal to the others?

A. $(a - b)^2$      B. $2a$      C. $(b - a)^2$      D. $6a - 2b$      E. $8a - 6b$

**EXAMPLE 8—**

If $x = 1$ and $y = -2$, then $2x - 3y =$

A. –7      B. –4      C. –1      D. 5      E. 8

**EXAMPLE 9—**

If M is the least positive integer for which 3M is both an even integer and equal to the square of an integer, then M =

A. 1/3      B. 3      C. 6      D. 12      E. 48

**EXAMPLE 10—**

If x and y are positive and even and $4 < x\,y < 16$, then $x - y$ could be _____?

**EXAMPLE 11—**

If $y = 3x$ and $x \neq 0$, then $3xy$ is

A. always positive     B. always negative
C. sometimes positive     D. sometimes negative
E. sometimes equal to zero

**EXAMPLE 12—**

8/M is an odd integer. Which of the following could be M?

A. 8/3     B. 5/8     C. 4/3     D. 2/3     E. 1/3

**EXAMPLE 13—**

If m/2 is even and m/4 is odd, then m could be

A. 32     B. 24     C. 20     D. 16     E. 10

**EXAMPLE 14—**

If $x + y = 2$, then $x + y - 3 =$

A. 5     B. 3     C. 1     D. –1     E. –3

# SOLUTIONS

**EXAMPLE 1—**

Pure substitution:

$(-3)^2(0) = 0$     $0/(-3) = 0$     $0 + 0 = 0$

Careful with zeroes.

**EXAMPLE 2—**

Trial and error. 0 works since $(0 - 4)^2 = (0 + 4)^2$. The answer is A.

**EXAMPLE 3—**

Again, trial and error. $x = 3$ and $y = 2$ satisfies both conditions. $x - y = 1$. The answer is A.

**EXAMPLE 4—**

Don't solve for x!!!! $5x = -3$. Soooo $(5x - 2)^2 = (-3 - 2)^2 = (-5)^2 = 25$.

**EXAMPLE 5—**

Trial and error is best. The answer is 9, 10, or 11.

Orr $2x < 24$; $x < 12$. $24 < 3x$; $8 < x$ or $x > 8$. The answer is 9, 10, or 11.

**EXAMPLE 6—**

M can't be B or D because a negative is always smaller than a positive. Also, numbers between 0 and 1, when raised to a power, get smaller. Therefore, the smallest even value for M is correct. A is the answer.

**NOTICE**

On this set, A occurs very often as the answer. Years ago, when test makers didn't know as much, C or D were the most common answers. Now, anything is possible. Let's go on.

**EXAMPLE 7—**

E is the only one where the answer is not 4. (It is −8.) Try to do this kind very quickly.

**EXAMPLE 8—**

Pure substitution. Be careful. $2(1) - 3(-2) = 2 + 6 = 8$. The answer is E.

**EXAMPLE 9—**

A, D, and E fit one condition, but A is not an integer and D is smaller than E. Answer, D.

**EXAMPLE 10—**

Again trial and error. x = 2 and y could be 4 or 6; x could be 4 and y could be 2; x could be 6 and y could be 2; x − y = −4, −2, 2, or 4.

**EXAMPLE 11—**

The answer is A, always positive, since the product of two positives or negatives is positive.

**EXAMPLE 12—**

B means 8/M is not even an integer. C, D, and E result in an even. The answer is A.

**EXAMPLE 13—**

m/2 is odd and m/4 even??? Only C satisfies both conditions.

**EXAMPLE 14—**

Do not solve for x or y. Substitute x + y = 2. x + y − 3 = 2 − 3 = −1. The answer is D.

This batch is not too bad. Let's try something else.

I believe with the change in exam and the use of calculators, this type of problem will increase a lot!!!! So, we will spend some time here. Most of these problems are short. The difficulty occurs because some of these questions are not done in school.

1. You must know how to compute, preferably without a calculator.

   a. $2^3 = 2(2)(2) = 8$      b. $3^{-4} = 1/3^4 = 1/81$

   c. $\dfrac{1}{5^{-2}} = \dfrac{1}{1/5^2} = 5^2 = 25$

2. a. $x^m x^n = x^{m+n}$      b. $x^6 x^3 x = x^{10}$
   c. $(3x^4 y^5)(-2x^{11} y^2) = -6x^{15} y^7$
   d. $x^{cats} x^{dogs} = x^{cats+dogs}$      e. $2^9 2^5 = 2^{14}$
   f. $x^8 x = x^{8+1}$

3. a. $x^m/x^n = x^{m-n}$      b. $x^{food}/x^{calories} = x^{food-calories}$
   c. $\dfrac{4x^4 y^5 z^6}{6x^9 y^5 z^2} = \dfrac{2z^4}{3x^5}$      d. $\dfrac{x^a x^c}{x^e} = x^{a+c-e}$

4. a. $(x^m)^n = x^{mn}$          b. $(x^5)^3 = x^{15}$
   c. $(5xy^6)^2 = 25x^2 y^{12}$      d. $(x^{4\ bananas})^{3\ bananas} = x^{12\ bananas^2}$

NOTES:

1b. Negative exponents mean reciprocal: nothing to do with negative numbers.

1c. Negative exponents in the bottom are positive exponents in the top.

2. When you multiply, if the base is the same, add the exponents.

2b, f. $x = x^1$.

2e. If the base is the same, add the exponents, buuut the base stays the same.

3. When you divide, you subtract exponents.

3c. $y^5/y^5 = 1$, and if the larger exponent is on the bottom, the answer is on the bottom: $x^4/x^9 = 1/x^5$. The 1 is not needed unless the top is all cancelled out.

3d. Combine 2 and 3.

4a. Power to a power? Multiply exponents.

4b. $(x^5)^3 = x^5 x^5 x^5 = x^{15}$.

5a. Fractional exponent: numerator is the power; denominator is the root.

5b. Alllways do the root first!

5.  a.  $n^{p/q}$        b.  $25^{3/2} = (\sqrt{25})^3 = 5^3 = 125$
    c.  $8^{-4/3} = 1/8^{4/3} = 1/(\sqrt[3]{8})^4 = 1/2^4 = 1/16$
    d.  $x^{a/b} x^{c/d} = x^{(ad + bc)/bd}$
    e.  $x^{2/3} x^{3/4} = x^{17/12}$        f.  $(x^{m/n})^{p/q} = x^{mp/nq}$
    g.  $(x^{3/4})^{7/5} = x^{21/20}$

6.  a.  $a° = 1, a \neq 0$        b.  $7° = 1$
    c.  $(3a)° = 1$        d.  $3a° = 3(1) = 3$

Basics are fairly straightforward. However, some of these can be a little tricky. Let's try some.

# LETS DO A BUNCH OF PROBLEMS

### EXAMPLE 1

The difference between $10^{60} - 10$ and $10^{59} + 10$ is closest to

A. 10    B. $10^2$    C. $10^{59}$    D. $10^{60}$    E. $10^{119}$

### EXAMPLE 2

$$\frac{a^{x+y}}{a^x} =$$

A. $a^y$      B. $1/a^y$      C. $-a^y$      D. $a^{1+y}$      E. $1 + a^y$

### EXAMPLE 3

$$\left(\frac{x^6 y^5}{x^3 y^2}\right)^2 =$$

A. $x^9 y^9$      B. $x^9 y^5$      C. $x^6 y^6$      D. $x^5 y^5$      E. $x^4 y^6$

### EXAMPLE 4

$$\frac{x^{2a+3} x^{4a+7}}{x^c} =$$

**EXAMPLE 5—**

If $3 = b^y$, then $3b =$

A. $b^{y+1}$    B. $b^{y+2}$    C. $b^{y+3}$    D. $b^{2y}$    E. $b^{3y}$

**EXAMPLE 6—**

$$\frac{1}{10^{29}} - \frac{1}{10^{30}} =$$

**EXAMPLE 7—**

$3^n + 3^n + 3^n =$

**EXAMPLE 8—**

If $\dfrac{a^{16}}{a^x} = \dfrac{a^x}{a^4}$, then $x =$

A. 8    B. 10    C. 6    D. 32    E. 256

**EXAMPLE 9—**

If $x^3 = 64$, then $x^{-2} =$

A. 1/4    B. 1/8    C. 1/16    D. $-4$
E. $-8$

**EXAMPLE 10—**

If $x > 0$ and $x^2 = 81$, then $x^{1/2} =$

A. 9    B. 3    C. $\sqrt{3}$    D. 1/3
E. 1/9

**EXAMPLE 11—**

If $(16^{3/4})^{5/3} = 4^x$,   then $x =$

A. 2.5    B. 3    C. 3.5    D. 4
E. 4.5

## HERE ARE THE ANSWERS

### EXAMPLE 1—

$10^{60} - 10 - (10^{59} - 10) = 10^{60} - 10^{59} - 20$

Factoring the first two terms, we get $10^{59}(10 - 1) - 20$ $\approx 9(10^{59})$, which is much closer to D, $10^{60}$. Subtracting 20 for a number this size is like subtracting nothing. (A million minus 20 is still about a million.)

### EXAMPLE 2—

This is hard only because some of you have never seen this in school. Now, it should be easy . . . $a^{x+y-x} = a^y$. The answer is A.

### EXAMPLE 3—

Simplify inside parentheses first: $(x^3y^3)^2 = x^6y^6$.     C.

### EXAMPLE 4—

The base is the same; when you multiply, you add exponents, and when you divide, you subtract exponents:

$$x^{2a + 3 + 4a + 7 - c} = x^{6a + 10 - c}$$

### EXAMPLE 5—

This is a problem that looks like it should be easy but is not:

$3 = b^y$

Multiply both sides by b!!!!

$3b = b^yb = b^{y + 1}$

The answer is A.

### EXAMPLE 6—

We have to go back to fifth grade and take a look at a problem:

$$\frac{7}{16} - \frac{3}{8}$$

How is this problem similar? You'llll seeee:

LCD 16 $\qquad \dfrac{7}{16} - \dfrac{6}{16} = \dfrac{1}{16}$

Let's look at it a different way. The LCD $= 16 = 2^4$.

$8 = 2^3 \qquad 2^4 = 2(2^3)$

Multiply the second fraction, top and bottom, by 2:

$$\frac{7}{2^4} - \frac{3}{2^3} = \frac{7}{2^4} - \frac{3(2)}{2^3(2)} = \frac{7-6}{2^4} = \frac{1}{2^4}$$

Sooooo, $\qquad \dfrac{1}{10^{29}} - \dfrac{1}{10^{30}} = \dfrac{1(10)}{10^{29}(10)} - \dfrac{1}{10^{30}} = \dfrac{9}{10^{30}}$

**EXAMPLE 7—**

A truly difficult problem. It is difficult because it is addition, not multiplication:

$3^n + 3^n + 3^n = 1(3^n) + 1(3^n) + 1(3^n) = 3(3^n) = 3^1 3^n = 3^{n+1}$

Fortunately, few are like this one.

**EXAMPLE 8—**

Cross multiply: $a^{2x} = a^{20}$. Then $2x = 20$ (equal bases, equal exponents), $x = 10$, and the answer is B!

**EXAMPLE 9—**

$x = 4$. Then $x^{-2} = 4^{-2} = 1/4^2 = 1/16$. The answer is C.

**EXAMPLE 10—**

$x = 9$. Then $x^{1/2} = \sqrt{x} = \sqrt{9} = 3$. The answer is B.

**EXAMPLE 11—**

A toughie. $16^{5/4} = (\sqrt[4]{16})^5 = 2^5$.  $4^x = 2^{2x}$.  $2^{2x} = 2^5$. $2x = 5$.  $x = 2.5$. The answer is A.

Need more info on exponents?   See *Algebra for the Clueless.*

## CHAPTER 9

# DISTRIBUTIVE LAW, FACTORING, REDUCING, ODDS AND ENDS

1. Let's do odds and ends first—**combining like terms:**

   a. $3a + 5b + 7a + 9b$      Answer: $10a + 14b$.
   b. $4x^2 - 7x - 9 + -7x^2 + 7x - 3$      Answer: $-3x^2 - 12$.

   In combining like terms, add or subtract; leave the exponents alone. Unlike terms, different letters, or the same letter(s) with different exponents, cannot be combined.

2. Next, the basic **distributive law:**

   a. $5(2x - 3) = 10x - 15$      b. $-2(5x - 7) = -10x + 14$
   (carrrreful of 2nd sign)      c. $4(5x - 3) - 7(4x - 1)$
   $= 20x - 12 - 28x + 7 = -8x - 5$

3. You need to be able to **multiply a binomial** kwikkkly by the F.O.I.L. method in your head!!! (F.O.I.L. = F = First, O = Outer, I = Inner, L = Last.)

   a. $(x + 5)(x - 3)$      First $x(x) = x^2$; Outer $x(-3) = -3x$; Inner $5(x) = 5x$; Last $(5)(-3) = x^2 + 2x$ (add inner and outer) $-15$

   b. $(x + 10)^2 = (x + 10)(x + 10) = x^2 + 20x + 100$

**45**

You must know these verrrry well. You'll see soon:

$. $(x + y)^2 = x^2 + 2xy + y^2$    $$. $(x - y)^2 = x^2 - 2xy + y^2$    $$$. $(x + y)(x - y) = x^2 - y^2$

You must know three kinds of factoring:

**NOTES:**

**4a. Largest number that multiplies 12 and 16 is 4; x is a factor of x and $x^2$.**

**4b. $x^2$ is a factor of $x^2, x^3, x^4$. If a whole term ($3x^2$) is factored out, a 1 goes in the parentheses.**

4. Take out the **largest** common **factor:**

   a. $12x^2 - 16x = 4x(3x - 4)$

   b. $9x^4 - 15x^3 + 3x^2 = 3x^2(3x^2 - 5x + 1)$

   c. $16a^2 \text{ bug} - 24a \text{ bug} = 8a \text{ bug}(2a - 3)$

5. Difference of 2 squares:

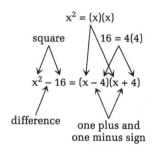

6. **Trinomials.** Verry important. We'll spend some time here because some of the newer and older books do not teach this properly. My way is the right way. Seriously, when I took algebra 400 years ago, all the teachers taught it this way. It still is the best way.

   $x^2 - 7x + 6$.    It factors into 2 binomials. Make 2 sets of ( ).

   Last sign + (+6), sign in each ( ) will be the same.

   Only if the last sign is +, look at the first sign.

   The first sign is minus (−7), which means both signs are minus (first plus, both plus).

Look at first term. $x^2 = x(x)$. Temporarily ignore the middle term.

$6 = 1(6)$ or $(3)(2)$. Factors must add to 7.

The correct answer is . . . $(x - 1)(x - 6)$, where the 1 and 6 could be switched.

$a^2 - 2a - 24$.      Last sign minus ($-24$), which means one sign in ( ) is + and one is −. $a^2 = a(a)$. $24 = 1(24) = 2(12) = 3(8) = 4(6)$. It must add to $-2$. 4 and $-6$.

$(a - 6)(a + 4)$ is the answer.

As most of you know, the first term doesn't have to be $x^2$. It could be $2x^2$ or $3x^2$, . . . but up to this point, if it happens, there is always a common factor, followed by a second factoring.

7. **Double factorings.**

   a.  $3x^2 + 9x + 6 = 3(x^2 + 3x + 2) = 3(x + 1)(x + 2)$

   b.  $2x^2 - 50 = 2(x^2 - 25) = 2(x + 5)(x - 5)$

   c.  $300 - 3a^2 = 3(100 - a^2) = 3(10 + a)(10 - a)$

If you need more help, you should get my *Algebra for the Clueless* or *Calc for the Clueless, Precalc with Trig for the Clueless* or the rest of the series.

8. **Reducing fractions.**

   a. $\dfrac{2x + 8}{2}$      Is it $x + 8$? Wrong! Is it $2x + 4$?

   Wrong! $\dfrac{2x + 8}{2} = \dfrac{2x}{2} + \dfrac{8}{2} = x + 4$, because of the order of operations.

   b. $\dfrac{x^2 - 4}{x^2 - 4x + 4} = \dfrac{(x + 2)(x - 2)}{(x - 2)(x - 2)} = \dfrac{x + 2}{x - 2}$

**NOTES:**

8a is the method with 1 term on the bottom.

8b is the method with 2 or more terms on the bottom.

## LET'S TRY SOME OF THESE

I don't know about you, but I can't wait!!!!!

### EXAMPLE 1—

The sum of $4(3x - 3)$ and $3(4x - 4) =$

A. 0    B. 24x    C. 24x + 24    D. 24x − 24
E. $144x^2 + 288x + 144$

### EXAMPLE 2—

If $x = b - 3$ and $y = b + 6$, then $x - y =$

A. −9    B. 3    C. −3    D. 9    E. 2b + 3

### EXAMPLE 3—

If $m^2 - n^2 = 18$, then $3(m + n)(m - n) =$

A. 6    B. 15    C. 24    D. 27    E. 54

### EXAMPLE 4—

If $y \neq 2$, then

$$\frac{y^2 + y - 6}{y - 2} - (y + 3) =$$

### EXAMPLE 5—

If $(g + 1/g)^2 = 40$, then $g^2 + 1/g^2 =$

A. 38    B. 39    C. 40    D. 42    E. 1599

### EXAMPLE 6—

$c^2 - d^2 + 2d(c + d) =$
A. $(c - d)^2$
B. $d^2 - c^2$
C. $c^2 + d^2$
D. $(c + d)^2$
E. $(d - c)^2$

### EXAMPLE 7—

If $a > 0$ and $a^2 - 1 = 41 \times 43$, then $a =$

A. 2    B. 40    C. 41    D. 42    E. 43

**EXAMPLE 8—**

The difference between $\dfrac{12a + 4}{4}$ and 3a is

A. 0     B. 1     C. 4     D. 6a + 1
E. 6a + 4

**EXAMPLE 9—**

$\dfrac{4a^2 - 4}{a - 1} = 4a + 4$ except when

A. a = 1     B. a = 1 or −1     C. a = 0
D. a = 0,1, or −1     E. It is never true.

**EXAMPLE 10—**

What is the result if 5 + 2a is subtracted from the sum
of 5 − a and $4a^2 + 5a + 6$?

**EXAMPLE 11—**

$(a + b)^2 = 25$ and $a^2 + b^2 = 1$;    ab =

A. 2     B. 4     C. 6     D. 12
E. 24

**EXAMPLE 12—**

a + b = m annnd a − b = 1/m, thennnn $a^2 - b^2 =$

A. 1/m     B. m     C. $m^2$     D. 2     E. 1

## LET'S LOOK AT THE ANSWERS!!

**EXAMPLE 1—**

Sum means "add." We get 12x − 12 + 12x − 12 =
24x − 24.     The answer is D.

**EXAMPLE 2—**

x − y = (b − 3) − (b + 6) = b − 3 − b − 6 = −3 − 6 = −9.
The answer is A.

**EXAMPLE 3—**

$3(m^2 - n^2) = 3(m + n)(m - n) = 3(18) = 54$.  The answer is E.

**EXAMPLE 4—**

Straight factoring (you must know how to do this):

$$\frac{(y + 3)(y - 2)}{(y - 2)} - (y + 3) = (y + 3) - (y + 3) = 0$$

**EXAMPLE 5—**

This is a realllly tough one:

$(g + 1/g)^2 = (g + 1/g)(g + 1/g) = g^2 + 2g(1/g) + 1/g^2$

$= g^2 + 2 + 1/g^2 = 40$

    $- 2$         $= -2$

Soooo $g^2 + 1/g^2 = 38$.  The answer is A.

**EXAMPLE 6—**

$c^2 - d^2 + 2d(c + d) = c^2 - d^2 + 2cd + 2d^2 = c^2 + 2cd + d^2$. Factoring we got D.

**EXAMPLE 7—**

You know $a^2 - 1 = (a + 1)(a - 1)$. You need to see $41 \times 43 = (42 - 1)(42 + 1)$. The answer is 42, D.

**EXAMPLE 8—**

$3a + 1 - 3a = 1$.  The answer is B.

**EXAMPLE 9—**

The bottom of a fraction can't be zero.    The answer is A.

**EXAMPLE 10—**

This would be a problem with choices, but it is really mostly a reading problem.

It says: Take $4a^2 + 5a + 6$, add $5 - a$, and then subtract $5 + 2a$ (*subtracted from* reverses the order because subtract 2 from 6 means $6 - 2$):

$$4a^2 + 5a + 6 + 5 - a - 5 - 2a = 4a^2 + 2a + 6$$

**EXAMPLE 11—**

$(a + b)^2 = a^2 + 2ab + b^2 = 25$; $a^2 + b^2 = 1$; subtracting, we get $2ab = 24$, or $ab = 12$. The answer is D.

**EXAMPLE 12—**

$a^2 - b^2 = (a + b)(a - b) = m(1/m) = \dfrac{m}{1} \times \dfrac{1}{m} = 1$. The answer is E.

Most of the algebraic problems are not too bad if you know your basic algebra.

Let's do some more. The next section is the part that most students like a lot, basic equations.

## CHAPTER 10

# EQUATIONS: ONE UNKNOWN

Let's do the basic types first. More later. The SAT seems to ask a lot of these. Most are not too hard.

Linear equations, first-degree equations, can get verrrry long. On the SAT they are almost all short or very short or very very short, sometimes a little tricky, sometimes truly easy. Here are a few samples.

**REMEMBER: You want to do as many steps as possible in your head!!!!**

## EXAMPLE 1—

$3x + 19 = 4$

$\phantom{3x} -19 = -19$

$3x \phantom{+19} = -15 \qquad x = -15/3 = -5$

## EXAMPLE 2—

$\dfrac{x}{3} + \dfrac{x}{2} = 4$ \qquad Multiply by LCD 6.

$2x + 3x = 24 \qquad 5x = 24 \qquad x = 24/5$

**EXAMPLE 3—**

$$\frac{4}{x} - \frac{2}{x} = 12 \qquad \text{LCD} = x \qquad 4 - 2 = 12x$$

$$12x = 2 \qquad x = 2/12 = 1/6$$

**EXAMPLE 4—**

$$x + 1 + x + 3 + x + 5 = 27 \qquad \text{Combine like terms.}$$

$$3x + 9 = 27 \qquad 3x = 18 \qquad x = 6$$

**EXAMPLE 5—**

If there are only two fractions . . .

$$\frac{7}{9} = \frac{x}{5} \qquad \text{Cross multiply.}$$

$$9x = 35 \qquad x = 35/9 \qquad \text{Better . . . in your head.}$$

$$x = 5(7)/9$$

Here's something more you might like to know if you have two fractions . . . (not in Example 5).

$$\text{If } \frac{a}{b} = \frac{c}{d}, \qquad \text{then} \qquad \frac{b}{a} = \frac{d}{c} \qquad \text{(flip)}$$

$$\frac{a}{c} = \frac{b}{d} \qquad \text{aaaannnd} \qquad \frac{d}{b} = \frac{c}{a}$$

In numbers, since 3/6 = 4/2, . . ., then 6/3 = 4/2 annd 3/2 = 6/4 annnd 4/6 = 2/3. Thththat's allll!!!

Seriously, there isn't too much more. However, the SAT sometimes is tricky. Let's try some.

# PROBLEMS

**EXAMPLE 1—**

If $a - 2 = 6 - a$, then $a =$

A. −4    B. −2    C. 2    D. 4    E. 8

**EXAMPLE 2—**

$3x + 11 = 50.$ $6x + 22 =$ what?

**EXAMPLE 3—**

$H \times 2/3 = 2/3 \times 5/9,$ $H =$

A. 5/9     B. 9/5     C. 5     D. 9     E. 14

**EXAMPLE 4—**

$\dfrac{2}{M} + \dfrac{2}{M} = 8.$     $M =$

A. 1/8     B. 1/4     C. 1/2     D. 2     E. 64

**EXAMPLE 5—**

If $5a = 6$ and $7b = 8,$ then $35ab =$

A. 4/3     B. 48/35     C. 35/48     D. 14     E. 48

**EXAMPLE 6—**

$4 \times 4 \times 4 \times 4 \times 4 = \dfrac{32 \times 32}{S}$     $S = ?$

**EXAMPLE 7—**

$5/a = 1$     $b/3 = 5$     $\dfrac{a + 3}{b + 4} =$

A. 8/19     B. 19/8     C. 2/5     D. 5/2     E. 4/9

**EXAMPLE 8—**

If $c - 5 = d,$ $c - 8 = d$ plus what?

A. 3     B. 13     C. −13     D. −3     E. 40

**EXAMPLE 9—**

⅓ of a number is 1 more than ¼ of the number. The number is

A. 3     B. 4     C. 12     D. 36     E. 144

**EXAMPLE 10—**

$$\frac{8}{5} = \frac{5}{x} \qquad x =$$

A. 8/25    B. 5/8    C. 8/5    D. 25/8    E. 200

# OK, LET'S SEE THE ANSWERS

**EXAMPLE 1—**

$a - 2 = 6 - a$

$2a = 8,$     so     $a = 4.$    The answer is D. Hopefully very easy for you.

**EXAMPLE 2—**

We double both sides: $x = 100$.

**EXAMPLE 3—**

It is as easy as it looks: 5/9, A. (The commutative law for those who want to be technical.)

**EXAMPLE 4—**

Multiply each term by M: $2 + 2 = 8M$, $8M = 4$, $M = 4/8 = \frac{1}{2}$.    The answer is C.

**EXAMPLE 5—**

Again, don't solve: $35ab = (5a)(7b) = 6(8) = 48$.    The answer is E.

**EXAMPLE 6—**

$$\frac{4 \times 4 \times 4 \times 4 \times 4}{1} = \frac{32 \times 32}{S}$$

Soooo    $\dfrac{S}{1} = \dfrac{\cancel{32}^{2} \times \cancel{32}^{2}}{4 \times 4 \times 4 \times 4 \times 4} = \dfrac{4}{4} = 1.$

Okay, okay, you might use a calculator here, but it still is much better if you could do this in your head.

**EXAMPLE 7—**

This one you have to solve. By cross multiplying,

5/a = 1/1    so    a = 5    b/3 = 5/1

So b = 15

$$\frac{a+3}{b+4} = \frac{5+3}{15+4} = 8/19.$$    The answer is A.

You must do enough of these to know the difference between Examples 5 and 7.

**EXAMPLE 8—**

c − 5 − 3 = c − 8.    The answer is D. This is not too bad.

**EXAMPLE 9—**

A reading problem:

$$\frac{1}{3} x = 1 + \frac{1}{4} x$$    ("Is" is the = sign.)

Multiply by LCD 12, every term!!!

4x = 12 + 3x    x = 12    The answer is C.

**EXAMPLE 10—**

Cross multiply: 8x = 25, x = 25/8.    The answer is D.

These are very important. Let's try some more.

## HERE ARE SOME MORE PROBLEMS

**EXAMPLE 11—**

If 2x + 9 = −14,    then  x =

A. −23    B. −23/2    C. −5/2    D. 5    E. 23/2

**EXAMPLE 12—**

$x + 7 = x + -b$      $b =$

A. 7      B. −7      C. −x      D. x      E. −2x + 7

**EXAMPLE 13—**

$$\frac{(20 + 50) + (30 + M)}{2} = 70 \qquad M =$$

A. 30      B. 40      C. 50      D. 60      E. 70

**EXAMPLE 14—**

$a + b$ is five more than $a − b$. Which has exactly one value?

A. a      B. b      C. a + b      D. a − b      E. ab

**EXAMPLE 15—**

I weigh 9 kg more than I did a year ago. My weight then was 9/10 of my weight now, how much did I weigh then?

A. 72      B. 81      C. 90      D. 99      E. 108

**EXAMPLE 16—**

$(8/9)y = 1$      $(4/9)y =$

A. 1/3      B. 1/2      C. 2/3      D. 3/2      E. 7/6

**EXAMPLE 17—**

A 50-cm piece is cut into 3 pieces: The first is 3 cm shorter than the second, and the third is 4 cm shorter than the first. The length of the shortest piece is

A. 10      B. 13      C. 15      D. 17      E. 20

**EXAMPLE 18—**

$$b = y + \frac{1}{3} = \frac{y + 2}{3} \qquad b =$$

A. 1/2      B. 2/3      C. 3/4      D. 4/5      E. 5/6

**EXAMPLE 19—**

If $5x - 3 = 4c,$     then $\dfrac{5x - 3}{2} =$

A. 9/4     B. 9/2     C. c     D. 2c     E. 4c

# OKAY, LET'S HAVE THE SOLUTIONS

**EXAMPLE 11—**

Straight algebra:

$2x = -23$     $x = -23/2$     The answer is B.

**EXAMPLE 12—**

Cross out x's from both sides because they are added. $7 = -b$. Multiply both sides by $-1$. $b = -7$.     The answer is B.

**EXAMPLE 13—**

Write 70/1 and cross multiply: $100 + M = 140$
$M = 40$     The answer is B.

**EXAMPLE 14—**

You might throw up your hands and say, "What do I do? What do I do?" Write something. Write what you read. $a + b = 5 + a - b$. The a's cancel. $b = 5 - b$. We could solve for b except we don't have to. The question asked is what can we solve for, not the answer. B (b) is the answer.

**EXAMPLE 15—**

Straight algebra, and not too easy.

$x =$ weight then     $x + 9$ is weight now

Weight then is 9/10 of weight now:

$x = 9/10(x + 9)$     Multiply by LCD, 10.

$10x = 9(x + 9)$

$10x = 9x + 81$        $x = 81$ kg

My weight then. Well, almost now. Mine is about 5 kg more as of this writing. Oh, by the way, the answer is B.

### EXAMPLE 16—

Do NOT NOT NOT solve for y. You should notice 4/9 is ½ of 8/9. ½ of 1 is ½.        The answer is B.

### EXAMPLE 17—

Let x = piece 2.  x − 3 = piece 1.  x − 3 − 4 = x − 7 is piece 3.

$x + x − 3 + x − 7 = 50$        $3x − 10 = 50$        $3x = 60$
$x = 20$

But this is NOT the answer.

We want the shortest piece!!!! x − 7 = 20 − 7 = 13. The answer is B.

Let's continue.

### EXAMPLE 18—

Multiply by 3. $3y + 1 = y + 2$.  $2y = 1$.  $y = ½$.  $b = y + ⅓ = ½ + ⅓ = ³⁄₆ + ²⁄₆ = ⁵⁄₆$.        The answer is E.

### EXAMPLE 19—

Divide by sides by 2; again we don't solve:

$$\frac{5x − 3}{2} = \frac{4c}{2} = 2c$$        The answer is D.

Enough of these already (although on the SAT most of us would like a lot of these). Let's try something else.

---

**NOTICE**

*Many of the answers on this page are B. It might happen or it might not.*

## CHAPTER 11

# EQUATIONS: TWO (OR MORE) UNKNOWNS AND QUADRATICS

When the SAT decided to allow calculators, certain problems couldn't be asked any more. Some things had to be added. Exponential questions were one, and this section was another.

You must know how to factor and solve basic quadratics.

**TYPE I**

Solve quadratics by factoring.

A. $x^2 - 2x - 15 = 0$.     Factor.

$(x - 5)(x + 3) = 0$.     Set each factor equal to zero.

$x - 5 = 0$   or   $x + 3 = 0$     $x = 5, -3$
(Last steps are better done in your head.)

B. $x^3 + x^2 = 6x$.     Get everything to one side.

$x^3 + x^2 - 6x = 0$     Factor. It's a cubic, degree 3, 3 answers.

$x(x + 3)(x - 2) = 0$     $x = 0, -3, 2$

**TYPE 2**

Solve for x by square rooting.

**NOTE:** This also can be solved by factoring: $x^2 - 49 = 0$, . . . but better by square rooting. Hooray for the square roots!

A. $x^2 = 49$.     Take ± square roots of both sides.

$x = \pm\sqrt{49}$     $x = +7$   or   $x = -7$

B. $5x^2 = 45$.     Divide by 5.

$x^2 = 9$     $x = \pm3$

**TYPE 3**

Solving two equations in two unknowns.

A.  By addition:

(1)  $x + y = 28$

(2)  $x - y = 4$     Add together.

$2x + 0 = 32$     $x = 16$     Substitute in Eq. (1) or (2).

$16 + y = 28$     $y = 12$

B.  By subtraction:

$4x + y = 18$

$x + y = 6$     Subtract.

$3x \quad = 12$     $x = 4$     Sooo  $y = 2$,    from Eq. (2).

I know, I know. As many of you know, there are many more types than those listed here. But up to this point, the SAT has asked only these. My books *Algebra for the Clueless* and *Precalc with Trig for the Clueless* may have more than you need or want.

# LET'S DO SOME PROBLEMS!!!!

**EXAMPLE 1**

$x + y = 5; x - y = 9; 4x =$

A. $-2$     B. $-4$     C. $-8$     D. $14$

E. $28$

**EXAMPLE 2—**

$x + y = 5; x - y = 9; 4y =$

A. $-2$     B. $-8$     C. $7$     D. $14$     E. $28$

**EXAMPLE 3—**

$x^3 + 2x^2 - 35x = 0.$     $x =$

A. $0$     B. $5, -7$     C. $-5, 7$

D. $0, 5, -7$     E. $0, -5, 7$

**EXAMPLE 4—**

$x^2 + 11x + 14 = 0.$     Which is the largest?

A. $x^2 + 11x$     B. $x(x + 11)$     C. $-14$

D. $0$     E. $14$

**EXAMPLE 5—**

If $x^2 = 4$, then $x^3 =$

A. $6$     B. $8$ only     C. $-8$ only     D. $6$     E. $8$ or $-8$

**EXAMPLE 6—**

The sum of two numbers is 26. The difference is 14.

   A. The larger number is 6.
   B. The larger number is 10.
   C. The smaller number is 10.
   D. The larger number is 26.
   E. The product of the numbers is 120.

**EXAMPLE 7—**

$(x + 2)(1/x) = 0$     $x =$

A. $2$     B. $0$     C. $-2$     D. $-2$ or $0$     E. any integer

**EXAMPLE 8—**

I buy a table tennis racket and one can of balls for $42.00. My friend buys the same racket and two cans of balls for $45. How much does a racket cost?

A. $39     B. $40     C. $41     D. $42     E. $45

$2a + 3b = 34$, $a + 2b = 14$, $\dfrac{3a + 5b}{2} =$

A. 20    B. 24    C. 36    D. 40    E. 48

# LET'S CHECK SOME OF THESE

**EXAMPLE 1—**

Adding we would get $2x = 14$. So $4x = 28$, E. Only the SAT would ask for $4x$ instead of $x$!

**EXAMPLE 2—**

Continuing Example 1, if $2x = 14$, then $x = 7$. Substituting we get $y = -2$.

So $4y = -8$; and the answer is B.

**EXAMPLE 3—**

A pure factoring problem! $x^3 + 2x^2 - 35x = x(x^2 + 2x - 35) = x(x + 7)(x - 5) = 0$. So $x = 0, -7$, and $5$. The answer is D. If you can't do this problem **easily**, you must get *Algebra for the Clueless*.

**EXAMPLE 4—**

I call this a "phony phactoring" or a "fony factoring." The question reaally asked, "Which is larger, $x^2 + 11x$ or 14?" If $x^2 + 11x + 14 = 0$, then $x^2 + 11x = -14$ since $-14 + 14 = 0$. A and B are the same. The answer is E since C and D are less than E.

**EXAMPLE 5—**

$x = \pm 2$. Soooo $(\pm 2)^3 = +8$ or $-8$.    The answer is EEEEE.

**EXAMPLE 6—**

$x + y = 26$. $x - y = 14$. Add: $2x = 40$; $x = 20$; $y = 6$. The product is 120, E.

### EXAMPLE 7—

$1/x$ is never $= 0$ since x is in the bottom. The answer is
$x = -2$,  C.

### EXAMPLE 8—

$r + 2b = 45$
$r +  b = 42$

Subtracting, the balls $b = 3$; racket $r = 39$.       The
answer is A.

### EXAMPLE 9—

Adding, we get $3a + 5b = 48$. So $(3a + 5b)/2 = 24$.
The answer is B.

These are fun or phun.

## LET'S DO SOME MORE!!!

### EXAMPLE 10—

If $x + y = 11$,    then  $2x + 2y =$

A. 13     B. 11/2     C. 22     D. 44     E. 88

### EXAMPLE 11—

$x + 2y = 4$; $2x + 2y = 6$. Which is the largest?

A. $x^2 + 7y$        B. $y^{20}$  C. $3x + 2y$        D. $10y$
E. $5x$

### EXAMPLE 12—

$b^2 = c^2$. Which must **not** *always* be $= 0$?

A. $b^2 - c^2$     B. $(b + c)(b - c)$      C. $(c + b)$
$(c - b)$     D. $b(b - c) - c(c - b)$      E. $b + c$

### EXAMPLE 13—

What are all solutions to the equation $x^2 - 4x = 0$?

A. 0     B. 4     C. –4     D. 0, 4     E. 0, 4, –4

**EXAMPLE 14—**

$\dfrac{x}{6} = x^2.$     I. $-1/6$     II. $0$     III. $1/6$

A. I only     B. II only     C. III only     D. II and III only     E. I, II, and III

**EXAMPLE 15—**

In a class of 60 students, the number of boys is twice the number of girls. Which of the following accurately describes the situation?

A. $b + 2g = 60$     B. $b - 2g = 0$     C. $2b - g = 0$
$\ \ \ b - \ \ g = 60$     $\ \ \ b + \ \ g = 60$     $\ \ \ b + g = 60$
D. $b + \ \ g = 60$     E. $b + 2g = 60$
$\ \ \ b + 2g = 0$     $\ \ \ b - 2g = 0$

**EXAMPLE 16—**

If $m^2 = 16$ and $n^2 = 36$, the difference between the largest value of $m - n$ and the smallest value of $m - n$ is . . .

A. 20     B. 10     C. 4     D. 2     E. $-2$

**EXAMPLE 17—**

$5m + 4n = 14$  and  $2m + 3n = 14.$  $7(m + n) =$

A. 7     B. 14     C. 21     D. 28     E. 35

**EXAMPLE 18—**

The area is 32. $a =$

A. 2     B. 4     C. 6     D. 8     E. 16

# NOW THE ANSWERS

### EXAMPLE 10—

$x + y = 11$. $2x + 2y = 2(x + y) = 2(11) = 22$.    The answer is C.

### EXAMPLE 11—

Subtracting and substituting, we get $x = 2$ and $y = 1$.

$A = 11$, $B = 1$, $C = 8$, and D and E are 10. Answer A is the biggest.

### EXAMPLE 12—

Only E is not always 0. Substitute $b = c = 5$.

Note: Sometimes, if you scan the choices first, the answer is there.

### EXAMPLE 13—

Factoring, we get $x(x - 4) = 0$, sooo $x = 0$ or 4.    The answer is D.

### EXAMPLE 14—

Not so easy. You must solve and ignore choices. Multiply by 6, and get everything to one side:

$6x^2 - x = 0$.   $x(6x - 1) = 0$.   $x = 0$    or    $6x - 1 = 0$. $6x = 1$.   $x = 1/6$.    The answer is D.

**You can also do this by substitution, but solving is probably a little better.**

### EXAMPLE 15—

Reading. You must be able to read.

$b + g = 60$.   $b = 2g$ or $b - 2g = 0$.    The answer is B.

With calculators, there will be more of these. I know it sounds cruel, but. . . .

**EXAMPLE 16—**

$m^2 = 16$  and  $n^2 = 36$.  $m = \pm 4$  and  $n = \pm 6$.

Max of $m - n$ is the largest m and smallest n. $m - n = 4 - (-6) = 10$.

Min of $m - n$ is smallest m and the largest n. $m - n = -4 - 6 = -10$.

The difference between the largest and the smallest is $10 - (-10) = 20$.     The answer is A.

I think this is a tough one, especially when you must do it and read it quickly. You must be careful.

**EXAMPLE 17—**

Adding, we get $7m + 7n = 7(m + n) = 28$. That's it.     The answer is D.

**EXAMPLE 18—**

The area of a rectangle is base times height.

$2a^2 = 32$.     $a^2 = 16$.     $a = 4$.     The answer is B.

**NOTICE**

*a can't be negative because on this planet, lengths are always positive. On another planet, you might be minus 5 feet 6 inches tall, but not on earth.*

Hey!!!! How did geometry sneak in here???? Sometimes the questions cross over two or more topics. Besides, we've done enough of these. Believe it or not, we've basically finished the algebra. Let's do some angles, then more on areas. Then a little more. And awaaaay we goooo!!!!

## CHAPTER 12

# GEOMETRY: FIGURE THE ANGLE

In doing an unofficial survey of about 40 SATs, out of 60 questions, an average of 12 or 20% of the math is geometry. Sometimes it is as low as 15% and sometimes as high as 25%. Therefore, geometry is verrry important. However, THERE ARE <u>NO</u> PROOFS. Here are some of the facts you need to know.

$\overline{AB}$ perpendicular to $\overline{CD}$ (notation $\overline{AB} \perp \overline{CD}$) means 90° angle. ∡ADC and ∡CDB are complementary angles because they add up to 90°. (Notice the spelling of *complementary*. A compliment is how beautiful or handsome you are.)

1.

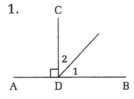

2.

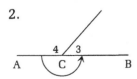

Angle ACB is 180°, halfway around the circle. ∡3 and ∡4 are supplements because they add to 180°.

3.

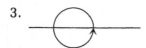

Once around a circle is 360°.

4.

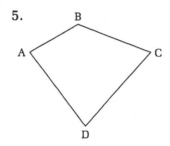

∢5 and ∢6 are vertical angles. They are equal. (I know, I know, in most of your geometry classes, they are "congruent," but not when I went to school. I am rebelling backward.) So are ∢7 and ∢8. Notice that ∢5 and ∢7 are supplements. So are ∢6 and ∢7, ∢6 and ∢8, and ∢8 and ∢5.

5.

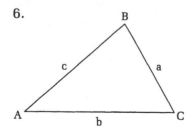

The sum of the angles of any quadrilateral (four-sided figure) is alllllways 360°.

6.

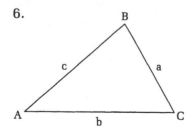

The sum of the angles of any triangle is . . . 180°.

Capital letters indicate vertices (points).

The side opposite A is little a.

The largest side lies opposite the largest angle.

So, if the figure were drawn to scale,

and $a < c < b$, thennnn

$\angle A < \angle C < \angle B$.

Angle x is called an EXTERIOR ANGLE, formed by one side of a triangle annnd one side of the triangle extended:

7.

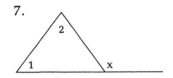

$\angle 1 + \angle 2 = \angle x$

8.

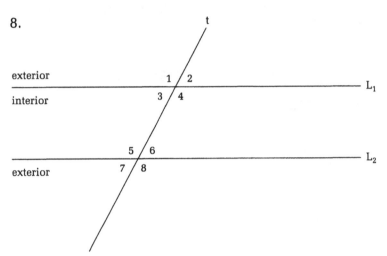

$L_1$ is parallel to $L_2$.

t = *transversal*, any line that cuts two or more lines.

$\angle 4$ and $\angle 5$, $\angle 3$ and $\angle 6$ are called *alternate interior angles* and are EQUAL.

$\angle 1$ and $\angle 8$, $\angle 2$ and $\angle 7$ are called *alternate exterior angles* and are EQUAL.

$\angle 2$ and $\angle 6$ (upper right), $\angle 4$ and $\angle 8$ (lower right), $\angle 1$ and $\angle 5$ (upper left), and

$\angle 3$ and $\angle 7$ (lower left) are called *corresponding angles* and are EQUAL.

$\angle 3$ and $\angle 5$, and $\angle 4$ and $\angle 6$ are called *interior angles on the same side of the transversal* and are SUPPLE-MENTARY (add to 180°).

Figure 8 revisited: Suppose you don't want to learn all of this. YOU DON'T HAVE TO:

All the angles less than 90° ($\angle 2$, $\angle 3$, $\angle 6$, $\angle 7$) are equal.

All the angles more than 90° ($\angle 1$, $\angle 4$, $\angle 5$, $\angle 8$) are equal.

Any two angles not equal must add to 180°. That's it!!!!

## LET'S DO SOME PROBLEMS

### EXAMPLE 1

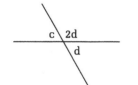

c =

A. 30°     B. 60°     C. 90°     D. 120°     E. 180°

### EXAMPLE 2

$L_1 \parallel L_2$. x + y =

### EXAMPLE 3

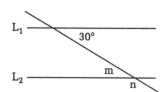

$L_1 \parallel L_2$. n − m =

A. 150°     B. 120°     C. 90°     D. 60°     E. 30°

### EXAMPLE 4

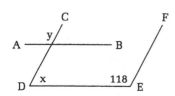

$\overline{AB} \parallel \overline{DE}$ annnnd $\overline{CD} \parallel \overline{EF}$. x + y =

A. 180°     B. 150°     C. 120°     D. 90°

E. can't be determined from the information given

**EXAMPLE 5—**

b − a =

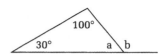

**EXAMPLE 6—**

L₁ ∥ L₂. b =

A. 30°     B. 40°     C. 70°     D. 80°     E. can't be
determined from the information given

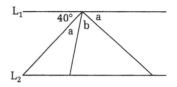

**EXAMPLE 7—**

y =

A. 40°     B. 42°     C. 50°     D. 58°     E. can't be
determined from the info given

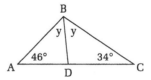

**EXAMPLE 8—**

b + c =

A. a/2 − 180°      B. 180° − a/2      C. 180° − 5a/2
D. 180° − a      E. a − 180°

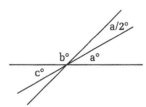

**EXAMPLE 9—**

The value of the middle angle is what?

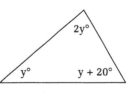

**EXAMPLE 10—**

(figure not drawn to scale)

y − 20° =

A. 40°     B. 50°     C. 60°     D. 70°     E. 80°

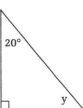

**EXAMPLE 11—**

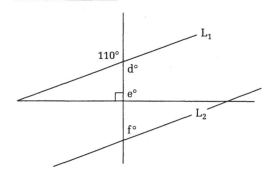

$L_1 \parallel L_2$.      $d + e + f =$

A. 180°      B. 220°      C. 230°      D. 270°      E. 330°

**EXAMPLE 12—**

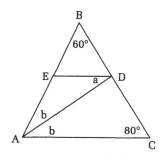

$\overline{DE} \parallel \overline{AC}$      $a =$

A. 70°      B. 50°      C. 40°      D. 30°      E. 20°

# HOW ABOUT SOME ANSWERS???? OK!

**EXAMPLE 1—**

$2d + d = 180°$ (supplements). $d = 60° = c$ (vertical angles).      The answer is B.

**EXAMPLE 2—**

x and y are clearly not equal. They must add to 180°.

**EXAMPLE 3—**

Angle m = 30° (alternate interior). n = 150° (sup).
$n - m = 120°$.      The answer is B.

**EXAMPLE 4—**

We only need to know that $\overline{AB}$ and $\overline{DE}$ are parallel and the two angles are not equal. They must add (like Example 2) to 180°.     The answer is A.

**NOTE**

If it says "cannot be determined," sometimes it can and sometimes it can't. It has been my observation that if it says "cannot be determined" twice on one SAT, both won't be "can't be determined," at least so far.

**EXAMPLE 5—**

$30° + 100° + a = 180°$. $a = 50$. $a$ and $b$ are sups. $b = 130°$. $b - a = 80°$.

**EXAMPLE 6—**

As much as you try, you can't find $b$. The answer is E. This may be the toughest of all because you must make a quick decision that it can't be determined.

**EXAMPLE 7—**

Easier than it looks. In the big triangle, $46° + 34° + 2y = 180°$. $2y = 100°$. $y = 50°$.     The answer is C C C!!!

**EXAMPLE 8—**

Look at the dark line. $a/2 + b + c = 180$. Soooo $b + c = 180 - a/2$.     The answer is B.

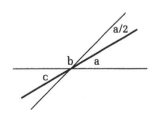

**EXAMPLE 9—**

$y + 2y + y + 20 = 180$. $4y = 160$. $y = 40$.

So $2y = 80$ and $y + 20 = 60$.     The answer is 60°.

**EXAMPLE 10—**

y is 70° (90 − 20). y − 20 is 50°. This doesn't look too hard if you have plenty of time. However, if you move quickly, as you must, you must READ this accurately.

**NOTE**

"Figure not drawn to scale" usually means two things:

1.  In a simple figure, it means it is not drawn to scale.

2.  In a complicated figure, it means it probably is drawn to scale even though it says it is not.

**EXAMPLE 11—**

d = 110° (vertical). e = 90° (sup of a rt angle). $L_1$ parallel to $L_2$. 110 and f not equal. They are sups. f = 70°. d + e + f = 110 + 90 + 70 = 270°.    The answer is D.

**EXAMPLE 12—**

Bigggg triangle ABC, 2b + 60 + 80 = 180. 2b = 40. b = 20. b = a (alternate interior).    The answer is E.

The first time I stopped here, I was tired. When I edited this for the first time, I ached from painting. Looks like this is the quitting page for me, but not for you. I'll pick this up tomorrow with more problems. But I really like these. My body doesn't seem to.

# PROBLEMS

**EXAMPLE 13—**

d + e = 3c. The value of d is what?

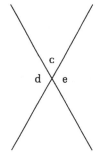

**EXAMPLE 14—**

$\overline{CD}$ bisects ∡ACB.  x =

A. 35°
B. 40°
C. 45°
D. 50°
E. 70°

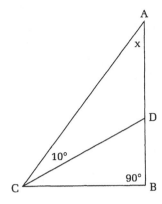

**EXAMPLE 15—**

∡ABC is 11x degrees. What can the value of x be?

A. 12     B. 8
C. 4     D. 2     E. 1

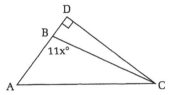

**EXAMPLE 16—**

b = 3a     c =

A. 30°
B. 60°
C. 70°
D. 80°
E. 90°

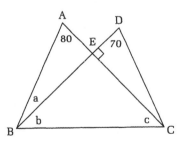

**EXAMPLE 17—**

(p + q + r) − (s + t + u) =

A. 0°     B. 45°     C. 90°     D. 135°     E. 180°

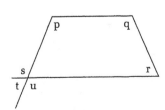

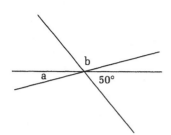

**EXAMPLE 18—**

b in terms of a is

A. 130 – a
B. 230 – a
C. 260 – 2a
D. 50 + a

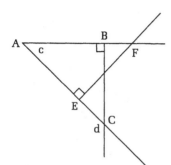

**EXAMPLE 19—**

d in terms of c

A. 90 + c
B. 90 + 2c
C. 180 – c
D. 180 – 2c
E. 2c

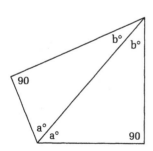

**EXAMPLE 20—**

a + b =

A. 30
B. 45
C. 60
D. 90
E. 180

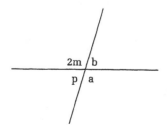

**EXAMPLE 21—**

180 – m =

A. m + a
B. m + p
C. a + p
D. a + b
E. p + b

**EXAMPLE 22—**

x + y + z =

A. 180
B. 210
C. 240
D. 270
E. 360

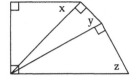

**EXAMPLE 23—**

w =

A. 10°
B. 12½°
C. 16°
D. 20°
E. cannot be determined from info given

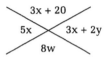

**EXAMPLE 24—**

y =

A. 30°
B. 33°
C. 36°
D. 40°
E. 45°

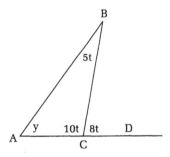

# OK, LET'S SOLVE THEM

**EXAMPLE 13—**

Since d = e, d + e = 2d = 3c. d = 3c/2.

d + c = 3/2 c + c = 180°. Multiply by 2. 3c + 2c = 360°; 5c = 360°; c = 72°.

d = 3/2 c = (3/2)(72°) = 108°.

**EXAMPLE 14—**

Angle ACB is 20° (double 10°). x = 70° since the sum of the angles of a triangle is 180°.

**EXAMPLE 15—**

Angle ABC is the exterior angle of triangle BDC and must be more than either interior angle, more than 90°. Only when x = 12, (12)(10) = 120°, can this happen.        The answer is A.

**EXAMPLE 16—**

This can be done quicker than it can be written. In triangle DEC, missing angle ECD is 20°, which you should probably write on your test paper. Angle AEB vertically equals 90°. In triangle ABE, the missing angle, a = 10°. b = 3a = 30°. Angle BEC is sup of 90°, which is 90°. b = 30°. Therefore, c = 60°.        The answer is B. Hmmmm. Maybe not quite trivial.

**EXAMPLE 17—**

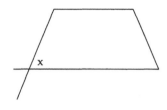

Labeling missing angle x, s + t + u + x = 360. p + q + r + x also = 360. s + t + u + x = p + q + r + x. Subtracting x, we see they are equal.

Sooo, subtracting one from another, the answer is 0°, A.

**EXAMPLE 18—**

b + vertical of a (= a) + 50 = 180. Sooo, b = 130 − a. The answer is A.

**EXAMPLE 19—**

Here is a typical example of what the SAT does. Line $\overline{EF}$ is there only to fool you. d is the exterior angle of triangle ABC. Focus on it. d = 90 + c.        The answer is A.

**EXAMPLE 20—**

$2a + 2b + 90 + 90 = 360$.      $2a + 2b = 180$.
$a + b = 90$.     The answer is D.

**EXAMPLE 21—**

$p + 2m = 180°$. $p + m + m = 180$. $p + m = 180 - m$.     The answer is B.

**EXAMPLE 22—**

The sum of the 9 angles of 3 triangles is 540. $540 - 4$ rt angles, $540 - 360 = 180 = x + y + z$.     The answer is A.

**EXAMPLE 23—**

Verrrry verrrry tricky. Lots of verticals. None should be used.

On top, $5x + 3x + 20 = 180$.  $8x = 160$.  $x = 20$.
$3x + 20 = 8w$.  $3(20) + 20 = 80 = 8w$.  $w = 10$.     The answer is A.

**EXAMPLE 24—**

Sups $10t + 8t = 180$. $18t = 180$. $t = 10$. $10t = 100$. $5t = 50$.
$y = 30°$.     The answer is A.

Most of these aren't too tough, and you must learn them because geometry is a substantial part of the SAT. But there is more.

This is a kind of problem that shows up every once in a while. When it does, it is always at the end of a test, one that if you worked out the "right" way, would take too long. It is the sum of "a lot of angles." I can't describe it any other way. All you need to know is the following (in triangles only):

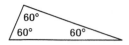

Let all interior angles = 60°, no matter what size.

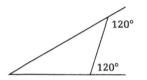

All exterior angles = 120°.

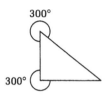

All "outside" angles = 300°.

Why will this work, especially when you know it's not true sometimes? Because if it is always true, it is true in the specific case when all the angles are equal. Why should you do it this way? The right ways will be too slow. What if I want to know the right way? Write me. I'll answer.

## PROBLEMS

### EXAMPLE 1—

$x + y + z - (a + b + c) = ?$

### EXAMPLE 2—

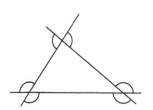

The sum of the 6 angles is what?

### EXAMPLE 3—

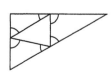

The sum of the 6 angles is what?

### EXAMPLE 4—

The sum of the 3 marked angles is what?

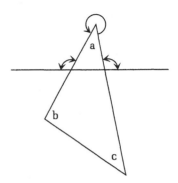

### EXAMPLE 5—

The sum of the 6 marked angles is what?

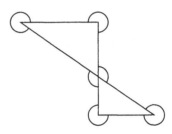

### EXAMPLE 6—

The sum of the 6 marked angles is what?

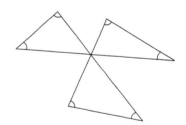

## SOLUTIONS

The trick solutions are very short. The real ones are not.

### EXAMPLE 1—

$3(120) - 3(60) = 180°$.

### EXAMPLE 2—

$6(120) = 720$.

### EXAMPLE 3—

$6(60) = 360$.

**EXAMPLE 4—**

$2(120) + 1(300) = 540$. The letters are there to fool you.

**EXAMPLE 5—**

$4(300) + 2(120) = 1440$.

**EXAMPLE 6—**

$6(60) = 360$.

They are always at the end of a section. With the trick, this is one right answer you probably would not get. But these problems rarely show up. Let's get back to more common ones.

## CHAPTER 13

# AREAL SEARCH

The SAT usually asks a number of questions on area.
Here are five formulas you should know, and two more
it would be nice to know.

**Rectangle**

$A = b \times h$

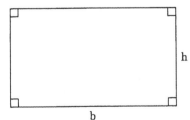

b = base   h = height

$A = 5 \times 7 = 35$ square units

**Square**

$A = s^2$

$A = 9$ squared = 81 square units

NOTICE

Squaring comes from a SQUARE!!!!!

**Circle**

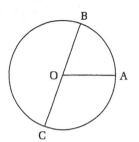

$\overline{BC}$ is a diameter.

$\overline{AO}$ is a radius.

$r = \frac{1}{2}d.$  $d = 2r.$

$A = \pi r^2.$

*Diameter:* Line segment from one side of the circle to the other through the center.

*Radius:* Line segment from the center to the outside, $\pi = $ approx 3.14.

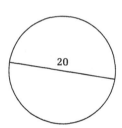

$d = 20.$

Sooo $r = 10.$

$A = \pi r^2 = \pi 10^2 = 100\pi.$

The answer on the SAT is almost always in terms of $\pi$.

**Triangle**

$A = \frac{1}{2}b \times h$

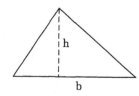

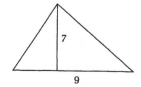

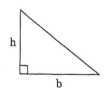

$A = \frac{1}{2} \times 9 \times 7 = 63/2 = 31.5$ square units.

### Sector

The shaded figure is called a *sector*. It is part of a circle. It usually is skipped, but it shouldn't be.

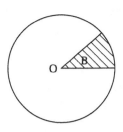

Center is O. What part of a circle, you ask? B/360.

So, the area of a sector is $(B/360) \times \pi r^2$.

$A = (40/360)\pi(6)^2 = 4\pi$ square units.

That's all there is, but it is important!

### Trapezoid

(nice to know because it shows up on the SAT)

$A = \frac{1}{2}h(b_1 + b_2)$
$h$ = height
$b_1$ = upper base
$b_2$ = lower base

Bases are parallel.
Other sides are not.
Bases are never equal.
Other sides might be.

$A = \frac{1}{2}h(b_1 + b_2) = \frac{1}{2}(8)(7 + 13) = 80$ square units

You really don't need to know this because trapezoids can be broken up into triangles and rectangles. But it is nice to know.

### Equilateral Triangle

$$A = \frac{s^2\sqrt{3}}{4}$$

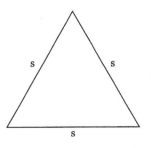

$$A = 9^2 \frac{\sqrt{3}}{4} = 81 \frac{\sqrt{3}}{4}$$

It's really important you know the areas. Sometimes the SAT asks more than one. Let's try some problems. Some are realllly innnnteresting.

## PROBLEMS

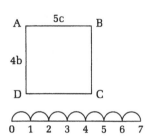

### EXAMPLE 1—

ABCD is a square; $16b^2 - 25c^2 = $ _____?

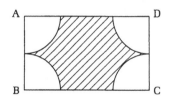

### EXAMPLE 2—

The area of the 7 semicircles is _____?

### EXAMPLE 3—

Rectangle ABCD, 4 arcs center at A, B, C, and D. $\overline{AD} = 12$. $\overline{AB} = 6$. Area of shaded portion is _____?

### EXAMPLE 4—

Circle center O. 3 equal semicircles. Area of large circle is $36\pi$. Area of the shaded portion is_____?

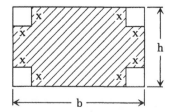

### EXAMPLE 5—

Area of the shaded portion is _____?

### EXAMPLE 6—

The length of rectangle C is 20% longer than rectangle D. The width of rectangle C is 20% less than rectangle D. The area of rectangle C is _____?

A. 20% greater than rectangle D

B. 4% greater than rectangle D

C. equal to rectangle D

D. 4% less than rectangle D

E. 20% less than rectangle D

**EXAMPLE 7**

Area of triangle ABC is 40. Area of triangle BCD is _____?

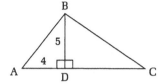

**EXAMPLE 8**

ABCD is a square. Area is

A. 9    B. 4    C. 1    D. ¼    E. cannot be determined from the info given

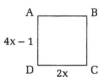

**EXAMPLE 9**

The area of the shaded portion is _____?

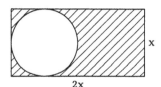

**EXAMPLE 10**

Center of the circle is O. Radius of the circle is 8. The total area of the shaded portion is $16\pi$. x =

A. 45    B. 90    C. 120    D. 135    E. 270

**EXAMPLE 11**

$\overline{XB} = \frac{1}{4}\overline{AB}$. Area of triangle CBX is 10. The area of rectangle ABCD is _____?

# LET'S LOOK AT SOME ANSWERS

**EXAMPLE 1**

Because it is a square, 4b = 5c. $(4b)^2 = (5c)^2$. $16b^2 = 25c^2$. They are equal. The difference is 0.

**EXAMPLE 2—**

Kinda tricky. Diameter of each semicircle is 1. Sooo, radius is ½. 3½ or 7/2 circles. Area is $7/2(\pi(\frac{1}{2})^2) = (7/8)\pi$.

**EXAMPLE 3—**

Area is 1 rectangle minus 4 (¼ circle) or 1 rectangle minus 1 circle, radius 3.

$$A = (12)(6) - \pi(3)^2 = 72 - 9\pi$$

**EXAMPLE 4—**

Picture is this.     You should see this.

½ large semicircle – ½ small semicircle.

Large circle is 36π. Radius is 6.

Area of semicircle is 18π.

Radius of smaller circle is (1/3)6 = 2.

Area of smaller circle is 4π.

Area of smaller semicircle is 2π.

$$18\pi - 2\pi = 16\pi$$

**EXAMPLE 5—**

This is a rectangle with 4 squares cut out: $bh - 4x^2$.

**EXAMPLE 6—**

Say rectangle D is 10 by 10 (remember, a square is a rectangle). Rectangle C would be 8 by 12 (20% longer by 20% shorter). 96, which is 4% less.     The answer is D.

**EXAMPLE 7**

Area of triangle ABD is ½(5)(4) = 10. Big triangle is 40. Right-most triangle is 40 − 10 = 30. You don't have to do anything else.

**EXAMPLE 8**

Square means $4x - 1 = 2x$. $2x = 1$. We don't have to solve for x since 2x is the side of the square!! $1^2 = 1$! The answer is . . . C, C, C.

**EXAMPLE 9**

Shaded portion isssss rectangle minus circle whose diameter is x. Radius is x/2:

$$A = bh - \pi r^2 = x(2x) - \pi(x/2)^2 = 2x^2 - \pi x^2/4$$

**EXAMPLE 10**

Area of the circle is $\pi r^2 = 64\pi$. The shaded part, $16\pi$, is ¼ of circle.

The unshaded part is 3/4 of circle.

3/4 of 360° = 270°      $2x = 270°$      $x = 135°$
The answer is D.

**EXAMPLE 11**

Really tricky and much easier than it looks. We can't find base or height, but we don't need to.

8 triangles make up the rectangle, which hopefully you can see without drawing: $8 \times 10 = 80$.

# LET'S TRY SOME MORE...

**EXAMPLE 12**

Area of the square with 2 sides tangent to the circle is $4b^2\pi$. The area of the circle is

A. $b\pi^2$    B. $b^2\pi^2$    C. $b^2\pi$    D. $2b^2\pi$    E. can't be determined

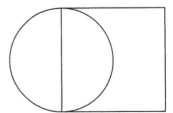

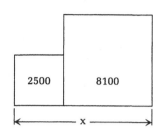

**EXAMPLE 13—**

Areas are given. Both are squares. x = ?

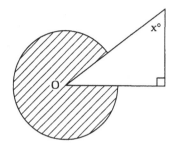

**EXAMPLE 14—**

Center of the circle is O. Radius is 10. Area of shaded portion is $80\pi$. x = ?

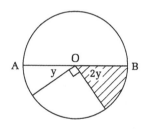

**EXAMPLE 15—**

Center is O. $\overline{AB}$ = 2. $\overline{AB}$ diameter. Area of shaded sector is

A. $\pi/12$    B. $\pi/8$    C. $\pi/6$    D. $\pi/4$    E. $\pi/3$

**EXAMPLE 16—**

The sum of the areas of 2 squares if the sides are 2 and 3, respectively, is

A. 5    B. 6    C. 10    D. 13    E. 25

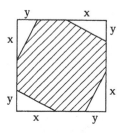

**EXAMPLE 17—**

The square has area of $4x^2$. If a rectangle with width x has the same area as the shaded portion, the length would be

A. $x - y$    B. $2x - y$    C. $x - 2y$    D. $4x - 2y$
E. $2x - 4y$

**EXAMPLE 18—**

The area of the rectangle and triangle are the same. cd/2 = 80. ab =

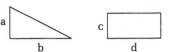

A. 320     B. 160     C. 80     D. 40     E. 20

**EXAMPLE 19—**

ABCD is a square, and the 2 shaded areas are semicircles. $\overline{AB}$ = 20. Find the ratio of the shaded region to the area of the square.

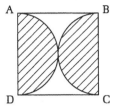

**EXAMPLE 20—**

Two circles have radius R + 2 and R. The difference in areas is 8π. The larger radius is

A. 1     B. 2     C. 3     D. 4     E. 9

**EXAMPLE 21—**

The area of the rectangle is 1. y =

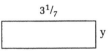

A. 7/22     B. 22/7     C. 3/7     D. 7/3     E. 7

# LET'S LOOK AT THE ANSWERS

**EXAMPLE 12—**

This is a very difficult one. $s^2 = 4b^2\pi$. Sooooo $s = \sqrt{\pi 4b^2} = 2b\sqrt{\pi}$. d = s. r = ½s = $b\sqrt{\pi}$. A = $\pi r^2 = \pi(b\sqrt{\pi})(b\sqrt{\pi}) = b^2\pi^2$.     The answer is B.

**EXAMPLE 13—**

A breather. Area of 1 square is 8100. Side is $\sqrt{8100}$ = 90. $\sqrt{2500}$ is 50. 50 + 90 = 140, which is the value of x.

**EXAMPLE 14—**

Another toughie. Circle radius 10 has area $\pi r^2 = 100\pi$. 80π/100π is 4/5 of the circle. The unshaded part of the circle is 1/5 of the circle and 1/5 of 360° is 72°. Angle x is 90 − 72 = 18°. Whew!!!!

## EXAMPLE 15—

$\overline{AO}$ is 1. Area is $\pi r^2 = \pi(1)^2 = \pi$. y + 2y + 90 = 180°. 3y = 90. y = 30°. 2y = 60°. 60°/360° = 1/6 of circle. The shaded portion is (1/6)π. C is the answer.

## EXAMPLE 16—

Another breather. Most of the SAT geometry is easy, but I've given you a larger example of the harder types. Getting back to this problem, $2^2 + 3^2 = 4 + 9 = 13$. The answer is D.

## EXAMPLE 17—

The square = shaded plus 4 triangles. Shaded = $4x^2 − 4(½)(x)(y)$. $4x^2 − 2xy$. Only on the SAT would you factor out only an x: $4x^2 − 2xy = x(4x − 2y)$.

If the width is x, the length must be 4x − 2y.    The answer is D.

## EXAMPLE 18—

Super tricky. cd/2 = 80. cd = 160 = area of rectangle = area of triangle = ½ab. So ab = 2(160) = 320.    The answer is A.

## EXAMPLE 19—

Area of square = $20^2 = 400$. $\overline{AB} = 20$ = diameter of circle (2 half circles). r = 10. Area is $\pi r^2 = \pi(10)^2 = 100\pi$. Ratio is 100π/400 = π/4.

## EXAMPLE 20—

$\pi(R + 2)^2 − \pi R^2 = \pi(R^2 + 4R + 4 − R^2) = 8\pi$    4R + 4 = 8
4R = 4    R = 1    R + 2 = 3    The answer is C.

**EXAMPLE 21—**

3½ y = (22/7)y = 1. y = 1/(22/7) = 7/22.        The answer
is A.

Enough of these; let's do perimeters!

## CHAPTER 14

# SECURING THE PERIMETER

When I went through this book for the first time, for some reason I left out all the perimeter formulas. Maybe that was because if it is anything other than a circle, the perimeter means merely adding up all the outside lengths. But let me list the formulas for those who absolutely must have formulas for everything.

Perimeter is 2b + 2h.
If you forget, add up all the sides.

Perimeter is 4s.
If you forget, add up all the sides.

Perimeter is a + b + c. h is NOT on the outside.

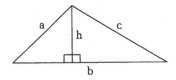

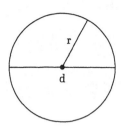

Perimeter of a circle is the circumference:
$c = \pi d = 2\pi r$

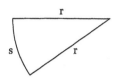

Perimeter is $2r + s$.
$r$ = radius; $s$ = arc length. The figure is a sector.

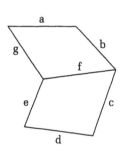

Perimeter is $a + b + c + d + e + g$.
$f$ is not part of the perimeter.

That's all there is to it.

## LET'S TRY SOME PROBLEMS

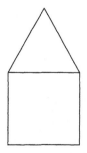

**EXAMPLE 1—**

This is an equilateral triangle with a square of area 100 underneath. The perimeter of the figure is

A. 30    B. 40    C. 50    D. 60    E. 300

**EXAMPLE 2—**

A square is divided into 4 smaller squares. The perimeter of the larger square is 2. The perimeter of the smaller square is

A. 1/8    B. 1/6    C. 1/4    D. 1/2    E. 1

**EXAMPLE 3—**

If the perimeter of square C is triple the perimeter of square D, the area of square C is how many times the area of square D?

A. 1/3    B. 1    C. 3    D. 9    E. 27

**EXAMPLE 4—**

X, O, Y, and Z are the midpoints of the diameters of the 4 semicircles. $\overline{CD}$ is a line segment containing the diameters of the semicircles. If $\overline{CD} = 12$, what is the length of the dotted line from C to D?

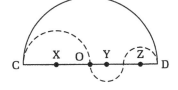

A. 6π    B. 12π    C. 18π    D. 24π    E. 72π

**EXAMPLE 5—**

$\overline{WX}$ and $\overline{YZ}$ are the diameters, length 10. Find the lengths of the darkened arcs.

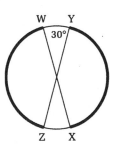

**EXAMPLE 6—**

A circle has circumference 1. The radius is

A. 2π    B. π    C. 1    D. 1/π    E. 1/2π

# OKAY, LET'S SOLVE THESE

### EXAMPLE 1

$A = s^2 = 100$. $s = 10$. There are 5 (not 6) 10s on the outside. $5 \times 10 = 50$.     The answer is C.

### EXAMPLE 2

If the ratio of the sides of a square (or any other figure) is ½, so are their perimeters: ½ of 2 is 1.     The answer is E.

### EXAMPLE 3

Suppose one square has a side s; its perimeter is 4s. A second square's side is 3s. Its perimeter is 12s. $12s/4s = 3/1$ (triple). The area of square 1 is $s^2$. The area of square 2 is $(3s)^2 = 9s^2$, 9 times the amount. The answer is D. (You could also use numbers, but make them verrrry simple.)

### EXAMPLE 4

The dotted line consists of 1 semicircle (medium semicircle) and 1 full circle (2 halves of the itsy-bitsy circle). If $\overline{CD} = 12$, $\overline{CO} = 6$, diameter of medium circle ½c $= ½\pi d = ½\pi 6 = 3\pi$. Itsy-bitsy circle has diameter 3. $c = \pi d = 3\pi$. $3\pi + 3\pi = 6\pi$.     The answer is A.

### EXAMPLE 5

The diameter of circle is 10. $c = 10\pi$. $30° +$ its vertical angle $30° = 60°$. The darkened arc is $360° - 60° = 300°$. $300/360 = 5/6$ of circle. 5/6 of $10\pi = 25/3\pi$.

### EXAMPLE 6

$$2\pi r = 1 \qquad \frac{2\pi r}{2\pi} = \frac{1}{2\pi}$$

So $r = ½\pi$.     The answer is E.

# LET'S TRY SIX MORE. . . .

**EXAMPLE 7—**

The perimeter is what?

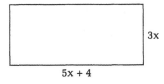

**EXAMPLE 8—**

A fence is 60 feet long in front of a building. There is a fence post every 6 feet.

The number of fence posts is what?

**EXAMPLE 9—**

A circle has center C. The area is 144π. The circle is divided into 6 equal parts. The perimeter of the shaded part issss

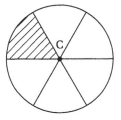

A. $24(1 + \pi)$     B. $12(2 + \pi)$     C. $4(\pi + 6)$     D. $4(\pi + 3)$
E. $12(1 + 2\pi)$

**EXAMPLE 10—**

If the perimeter of a 7-sided figure is 15, and each side is lengthened by 3 units, the perimeter of the new figure is?

**EXAMPLE 11—**

The perimeter of a rectangle is 100. What could one of the values of the sides be?

I. 45     II. 50     III. 55

A. I only     B. II only     C. III only     D. I and II
E. II and III

**EXAMPLE 12—**

What is half the perimeter of a square if the area is 64?

## LET'S CHECK OUT THE RESULTS

### EXAMPLE 7—

This is a straight perimeter problem:

$5x + 4 + 5x + 4 + 3x + 3x = 16x + 8$

### EXAMPLE 8—

A trick question. 60 divided by 6 is 10, buuuut you need a fence post at the beginning. So we need 11 fence posts.

### EXAMPLE 9—

Semicomplicated, but it shouldn't be too hard:

$A = \pi r^2 = 144\pi$      $r^2 = 144$      $r = 12$
c (of whole circle) is $2\pi r = 2\pi(12) = 24\pi$

This sector is 1/6 of a circle. Soooo

$\text{arc} = (1/6)24\pi = 4\pi$

The perimeter is $4\pi + 2$ radii $= 4\pi + 24 = 4(\pi + 6)$. C is the one, is the one, is the one.

### EXAMPLE 10—

You do not have to know the length of each side. If 3 units are added to each side, $3 \times 7 = 21$. $21 + 15 = 36$.

### EXAMPLE 11—

If one side is 45, then two sides would add to 90; the other sides would be 5 and 5. It is possible. If one side is 50, $50 + 50 = 100$. Other sides would be 0 and 0, not possible. $55 + 55 = 110$, clearly not possible. A is the answer.

**EXAMPLE 12—**

If you had a lot of time, this problem would be very easy. But when time is short, you must read quickly and accurately:

$s^2 = 64$     $s = 8$     ½ the perimeter, 2s, is 16.

# LET'S DO A FEW MORE EXAMPLES

### EXAMPLE 13—

RSTU is a rectangle with 16 semicircles as shown. The total arc length is 16π.

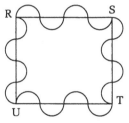

1. What is the area of rectangle RSTU?

2. For fun, what is the area inside the curved region bounded by all the semicircles from R to S to T to U and back to R?

### EXAMPLE 14—

A circle of radius 10 rolls on a 500-foot line. How many revolutions does it make?

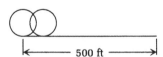

### EXAMPLE 15—

If each line segment represents a fence on a farm that is divided into 4 equal regions, what is the total length of the fencing needed?

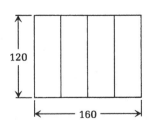

## LET'S CHECK THESE NOW

**EXAMPLE 13—**

16 semicircles = 8 circles = $8\pi d = 16\pi$. So $d = 2$.

Each side of the rectangle (actually a square) is 8. $8 \times 8 = 64$, the area. The answer is B. Surprisingly, this part is now very easy. The area of the rectangle is <u>exactly</u> the area inside the regions, since for each semicircle inside, there is one outside. So the area is also 64. This is quite difficult to see in a short period of time, but that is one of the reasons I wrote this book: to show you what to look for so that you can see the picture quickly, verry quickly.

**EXAMPLE 14—**

Revolution = 1 circumference = $\pi d = 20\pi$ feet per revolution.

Total length is 500 feet.

Revolutions $= \dfrac{500}{20\pi} = \dfrac{25}{\pi}$ revolutions.

**EXAMPLE 15—**

This is not too bad. $2(160) = 320$. $5(120) = 600$. $600 + 320 = 920$ feet of fencing.

Let's look at old Pythagoras and perhaps the most famous theorem in all of math!!!!

## CHAPTER 15

# OLD PYTHAGORAS (AND A LITTLE ISOSCELES)

The SAT has grown to ask many more questions about old Pythag. Most theorems have only one or two proofs. There are over 100 distinct proofs of this theorem. Here are the facts, just the facts.

**Right Triangle.**
Side c is the *hypotenuse*, opposite the right angle C. Sides a and b are called *legs*. In a *right triangle*, $c^2 = a^2 + b^2$. Of the original proofs, three were contributed by past presidents of the United States. We actually had presidents who knew and really cared about math!!!! Probably never again! A shame!!!!

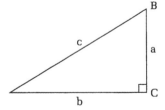

EXAMPLE 1

$$x^2 = 5^2 + 7^2 = 74 \qquad x = \sqrt{74}$$

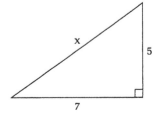

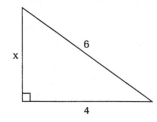

**EXAMPLE 2—**

$x^2 + 4^2 = 6^2$      (Hypotenuse is allllways by itself.)

$x^2 + 16 = 36$

$x^2 = 20$

$x = \sqrt{20} = 2\sqrt{5}$

## Isosceles Triangle

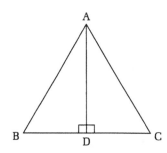

Equal sides (2), $\overline{AB} = \overline{AC}$, are called *legs*. Angle BAC is a *vertex angle*. Base $\overline{BC}$ can be bigger than, equal to, or less than each leg. Base angle B = base angle C. $\overline{AD}$, altitude, divides the base in half.

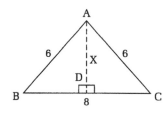

**EXAMPLE 3—**

Find the height x and the area of the triangle. (SAT likes this picture.)

$\overline{AD}$ wasn't originally given. If you draw it, $\overline{BD} = 4$. If you notice, this is Example 2: $x = 2\sqrt{5}$.

$A = \frac{1}{2}b \times h = \frac{1}{2} \times 8 \times 2\sqrt{5} = 8\sqrt{5}$ square units.

There are special right triangles the SAT loves. You must know them. I believe as the years go on they will show up more and more. As a bonus, for those of you who take geometry (most of you) and trig (hopefully more of you), they are a must!!

The exact *Pythagorean triples* (the most important ones):

1. The 3-4-5 group ($3^2 + 4^2 = 5^2$) 3, 4, 5      6, 8, 10
   9, 12, 15      12, 16, 20      15, 20, 25

2. The 5-12-13 group ($5^2 + 12^2 = 13^2$)
   5, 12, 13   10, 24, 26

3. The 8-15-17 group $(8^2 + 15^2 = 17^2)$   8, 15, 17

4. The 7-24-25 group $(7^2 + 24^2 = 25^2)$   7, 24, 25

If you are really bad at memorization, know these at least:

3, 4, 5     6, 8, 10     and     5, 12, 13

There are two others that are vital. The first, the **45-45-90 isosceles right triangle,** is one of the SAT absolute favorites.

Legs are equal:

1. From leg to hypotenuse, multiply by $\sqrt{2}$.

2. From hypotenuse to leg, divide by $\sqrt{2}$.

### EXAMPLE A—

Legs are equal. Soooo x = 7.

y, the hypotenuse $= x\sqrt{2} = 7\sqrt{2}$

That's it.

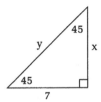

### EXAMPLE B—

Hypotenuse to leg???? Divide by $\sqrt{2}$.

Leg $x = y = \dfrac{8}{\sqrt{2}} = \dfrac{8\sqrt{2}}{\sqrt{2}\sqrt{2}} = \dfrac{8\sqrt{2}}{2} = 4\sqrt{2}$

This is not too hard, but knowing this is vital. We need to know one more triangle.

The second is the **30°-60°-90° right triangle.**
Short leg is always opposite the 30° angle.
Long leg is alllways opposite the 60° angle.
Hypotenuse, the longest side, is always opposite the 90° angle.

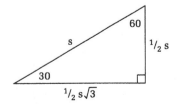

1. Always get the short leg first if it is not given!!!

2. Short to hypotenuse, multiply by 2.

3.  Hypotenuse to short, divide by 2.

4.  Short to long, multiply by $\sqrt{3}$.

5.  Long to short, divide by $\sqrt{3}$.

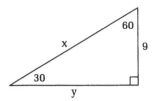

### EXAMPLE C—

Short is given.

Short to hypotenuse, multiply by 2. $9(2) = 18$.

Short to long, multiply by $\sqrt{3}$. $9(\sqrt{3}) = 9\sqrt{3}$:

$x = 18 \qquad y = 9\sqrt{3}$

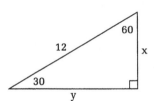

### EXAMPLE D—

Hypotenuse is given. Find short first.

Hypotenuse to short, divide by 2. $12/2 = 6$.

Short to long, multiply by 3. $6\sqrt{3}$:

$x = 6 \qquad y = 6\sqrt{3}$

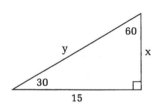

### EXAMPLE E—

Long given. Get short first.

Long to short, divide by 3:

$$\frac{15}{\sqrt{3}} = \frac{15\sqrt{3}}{\sqrt{3}\sqrt{3}} = \frac{15\sqrt{3}}{3} = 5\sqrt{3}$$

Short to hypotenuse, multiply by 2:

$2(5\sqrt{3}) = 10\sqrt{3} \qquad x = 5\sqrt{3} \qquad y = 10\sqrt{3}$

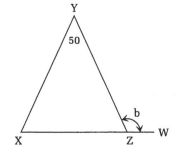

**PROBLEMS INVOLVING THESE TRIANGLES ARE <u>VERY</u> EASY IF YOU KNOW THESE FACTS COLD. YOU MUSSSSTTTT KNOW THESE WELL!!!!**

## LET'S DO SOME PROBLEMS

### EXAMPLE 1—

$\overline{XY} = \overline{YZ}$. $b = ?$

**EXAMPLE 2—**

HJKM is a square. The area of this square is what?

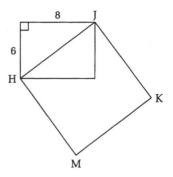

**EXAMPLE 3—**

A 25-foot ladder is placed against a vertical wall with the bottom of the ladder standing 7 feet from the base of the building. If the top of the ladder slips down 9 feet, then how far will the bottom slip?

A. 10 feet    B. 13 feet    C. 15 feet    D. 17 feet
E. 20 feet

**EXAMPLE 4—**

3 squares. $\overline{WX}$ is a line segment forming the diagonals of both smaller squares.

The ratio of $\dfrac{\text{length of } \overline{WX}}{\text{length of } \overline{YZ}} =$

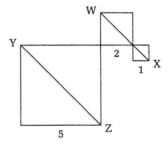

**EXAMPLE 5—**

Arc AB is ¼ of the circumference of the circle. Chord $\overline{AB}$ is y. What is the diameter of the circle?

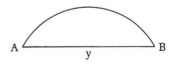

# LET'S SHOW SOME SOLUTIONS

**EXAMPLE 1—**

A relatively mild one to start. Angles X and XZY are equal because it is an isosceles triangle. Call the angle a.

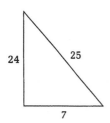

$2a + 50 = 180$      $2a = 130$      $a = 65$
a and b are sups      $b = 180 - 65 = 115$

### EXAMPLE 2—

If you know your Pythag trips, this is trivial: 6, 8, . . . , 10!!!! $10^2 = 100$.

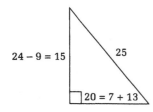

### EXAMPLE 3—

If you know your trips <u>very well</u>, this is not too bad.

$x = 20$      (15, 20, 25 triple)

$20 - 7 = 13$

The answer is B.

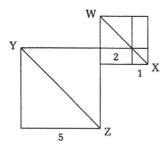

### EXAMPLE 4—

A real trick. You do NOT *need* to know there are 45-45-90 triangles. Imagine that WX is the diagonal of a square that contains the smaller two squares. The ratio of the diagonals is the same as the ratio of the sides. The answer is just 3/5.

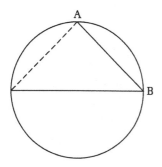

### EXAMPLE 5—

A tricky, tricky problem. If you actually drew the arc in a circle, you would see it forms a 45-45-90 right triangle whose sides are y, y, and $y\sqrt{2}$, which is the diameter. $y\sqrt{2}$ is the answer.

You really have to know these triangles well, as you must know all the formulas, even though many are put at the top of the SAT. If you need to look, you are already in trouble.

# LET'S DO SOME MORE!!!!

### EXAMPLE 6—
$\overline{BD}$ is $\sqrt{8}$. The area of the 4 semicircles is what?

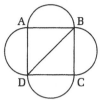

### EXAMPLE 7—
The value of x is what?

### EXAMPLE 8—
$\overline{PQ} = \overline{QT} = \overline{TR} = \overline{RS}$. Angle y = ?

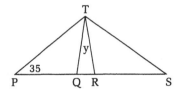

### EXAMPLE 9—
$\overline{AB} = 6\sqrt{2}$. Area of shaded region is what?

### EXAMPLE 10—
UVWX is a square. $2\overline{YW} = \overline{VY}$. Angle a = ? degrees.

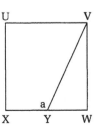

# LET'S SEE THE RESULTS

### EXAMPLE 6—
ABD is a 45-45-90 right triangle, hypotenuse $\overline{BD}$. $\overline{AB}$, the diameter of the semicircle = $\sqrt{8}/\sqrt{2} = \sqrt{4} = 2$.

Radius of semicircle is 1.

4 semicircles = 2 circles = $2 \times \pi(1)^2 = 2\pi$.

### EXAMPLE 7—

$x = \sqrt{6^2 - 3^2} = \sqrt{27}$. If you are really clever, you might see that this is a 30-60-90 right triangle. Opposite the 60° angle is the short side, 3, times the square root of 3. The answer is $3\sqrt{3}$, which is the same as $\sqrt{27}$.

### EXAMPLE 8—

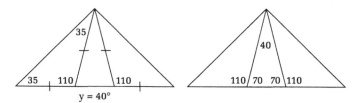

### EXAMPLE 9—

The SAT really likes this picture, really really, really.

$\overline{AO}$ is the leg of a 45-45-90 right triangle and is $6\sqrt{2}/\sqrt{2} = 6$. The area of the shaded region is the area of ¼ circle minus the area of the triangle, where r = 6, b = 6, and, I know it's boring, but h = 6 also. The area of shaded region is

$$\tfrac{1}{4}\pi r^2 - \tfrac{1}{2}bh = \tfrac{1}{4}\pi(6)^2 = \tfrac{1}{2}(6)(6) = 9\pi - 18$$

### EXAMPLE 10—

We have a 30-60-90 triangle. So angle WVY = 30°. So, angle VYW is 60°. a is the supplement = 120°.

I think we need some more. Remember geometry is about 20% of the SAT.

## LET'S TRY SOME

### EXAMPLE 11—

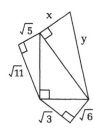

$y^2 - x^2 = ?$

**EXAMPLE 12—**

$\overline{XY} \parallel \overline{OZ}$.      The area of XYZO is

A. 12      B. 20      C. 30      D. 42
E. can't be determined

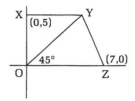

**EXAMPLE 13—**

$\dfrac{y}{4} = ?$

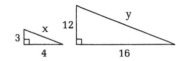

**EXAMPLE 14—**

a = ?

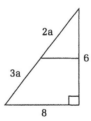

**EXAMPLE 15—**

The difference between the hypotenuse of a right
triangle whose legs are 5 and 12 and the hypotenuse
of a right triangle whose legs are 6 and 8 is what?

# OK, LET'S SEE THE ANSWERS

**EXAMPLE 11—**

$z^2 = y^2 - x^2$.

But $z^2$ also $= a^2 + b^2$.

Buut $a^2 = (\sqrt{11})^2 + (\sqrt{5})^2 = 16$. $b^2 = (\sqrt{3})^2 + (\sqrt{6})^2 = 9$.

$a^2 + b^2 = y^2 - x^2 = 9 + 16 = 25$.

When you see it, it takes much longer to write out than
to do.

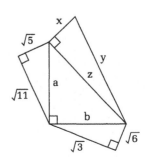

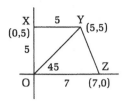

**EXAMPLE 12—**

45° angle. $\overline{OX} = 5$. So $\overline{XY} = 5$ (also on a 45° line x = y, which we'll look at a little later).

Area of trapezoid = ½h(b$_1$ + b$_2$)    h = 5    b$_1$ = 5
b$_2$ = 7    ½(5)(5 + 7) = 30
The answer is C.

The problems could be also done by finding the area of the two triangles and adding, but this is better!!

**EXAMPLE 13—**

There are two ways to do this problem. x = 5, a 3, 4, 5 right triangle. y = 4x = 20. So, y/4 = 5. 12, 16, 20 is also a triple. y = 20; so y/4 = 5.

**EXAMPLE 14—**

Easy if you know the triple, 6, 8, . . . ,10. 2a + 3a = 10. a = 2.

**EXAMPLE 15—**

Another question on Pythag's triples. 13 − 10 = 3.

# OK, A FEW MORE. . .

**EXAMPLE 16—**

$\overline{CD}$ is 6    $\overline{BD} = 3$

Perimeter of the shaded region is what?

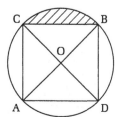

**EXAMPLE 17—**

A right triangle has sides 1 and $\sqrt{2}$. What can the third side be?

I. 1     II. $\sqrt{2}$     III. $\sqrt{3}$

A. I only     B. II only     C. III only
D. I and II only     E. I and III only

**EXAMPLE 18—**

Area of the semicircle is what?

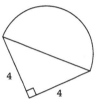

**EXAMPLE 19—**

The ratio of $\overline{NP}$ to $\overline{MN}$ is

A. $\sqrt{2}-1$     B. $\sqrt{2}/2$     C. $\sqrt{2}$     D. $\sqrt{2}+1$     E. $2\sqrt{2}$

Last set (last set of this type).

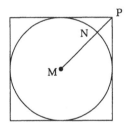

**EXAMPLE 20—**

In the figure, $\triangle ABC$ and $\triangle DEF$ are equilateral. If $\overline{DE} = 24$, the perimeter of $\triangle ABC =$

A. 24     B. 36     C. 48     D. $12\sqrt{3} \approx 20.78$
E. $24\sqrt{3} \approx 41.56$.

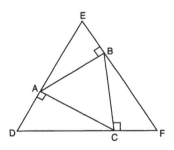

**EXAMPLE 21—**

The hypotenuse of a right triangle is 10, and a and b are the legs. If $a < 6$, which of the following describes all values of b?

A. $0 < b < 4$     B. $4 < b < 6$     C. $6 < b < 8$
D. $8 < b < 10$     E. $10 < b < 16$

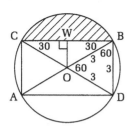

## LET'S LOOK AT THE ANSWERS

### EXAMPLE 16—

Tough problem! Lots of little things in the picture. It can be done quickly if you see the pieces. $\overline{CD} = 6$ (diameter). $\overline{CO} = \overline{OB}$ = radius = 3. So the right-most triangle is equilateral. All angles 60°. So angle OBW = angle WCO = 30°. So angle COW (moooo) = 60°. So triangle COW (mooo again) is a 30-60-90 triangle:

$$\overline{CO} = 3 \qquad \overline{WO} = 1.5 \qquad \overline{CW} = 1.5\sqrt{3}$$
$$\overline{CB} = 2\overline{CW} = 3\sqrt{3}$$

Arc CB is 120°. 120/360 = ⅓ of circumference. ⅓(6π) = 2π. Total perimeter is $2\pi + 3\sqrt{3}$.

### EXAMPLE 17—

$$x = 1 \qquad 1^2 + 1^2 = (\sqrt{2})^2$$

Since 1 and 1 are usually 2, I is true.

$x = \sqrt{2}$ can't work no matter what order you try.

$x = \sqrt{3}$ works since $1^2 + (\sqrt{2})^2 = (\sqrt{3})^2$ since 1 + 2 is usually 3. The answer is E.

### EXAMPLE 18—

Hypotenuse = diameter of semicircle is $4\sqrt{2}$(45-45-90 right triangle).

$$r = 2\sqrt{2} \qquad A = \pi r^2 = \pi(2\sqrt{2})^2 = 8\pi$$

Area of half a circle is ½πr² = ½8π = 4π.

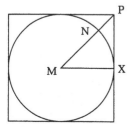

### EXAMPLE 19—

This is truly a tough one, but the reason the problem is here is there is a sneaky way around it.

Let's do it the "right" way and the SAT way:

Let $\overline{MX}$ = 1. (You must know to draw $\overline{MX}$.) $\overline{XP}$ = 1 (45-45-90 leg).

$\overline{MP} = \sqrt{2}$. (45-45-90 hypotenuse.) $\overline{MN}$ is another radius = 1.

$\overline{NP} = \overline{MP} - \overline{MN} = \sqrt{2} - 1$. $\overline{NP}/\overline{MN} = \sqrt{2} - 1 / 1 = \sqrt{2} - 1$. The answer is A.

If you can do this, then you probably didn't need to buy this book. But suppose you can't do this. . . .

We can measure the ratio between $\overline{NP}$ and $\overline{MN}$. Mark off $\overline{NP}$ on a pencil or scrap of paper. Then measure $\overline{MN}$. You see that $\overline{MN}$ is a little more than twice $\overline{NP}$. So $\overline{NP}/\overline{MN}$ is a little less than ½. Let's look at the choices knowing that $\sqrt{2}$ = approx 1.4 ($\sqrt{3}$ = approx 1.7).

E. $2\sqrt{2} = 2(1.4)$ certainly is not less than ½.

D. $\sqrt{2} + 1 = 1.4 + 1$ surely is not less than ½.

C. $\sqrt{2} = 1.4$, nope.

B. $\sqrt{2} / 2$ is about 0.7.

Possibly, we could have measured wrong, but $\sqrt{2} - 1 = 1.4 - 1 = .4$, yay, the correct answer. With choices, there sometimes is a trick like this.

**EXAMPLE 20—**

$\triangle ACD$ and $\triangle BAE$ (and also $\triangle BCF$) are all congruent 30°, 60°, 90° triangles. $2\overline{AD} = \overline{DC} = \overline{AE}$. If we let x = $\overline{AD}$, then $\overline{DE} = \overline{AD} + \overline{AE} = x + 2x = 3x = 24$. So $\overline{AD}$ = 8. $\overline{AC} = \overline{AD}\sqrt{3} = 8\sqrt{3}$. Finally, the perimeter of $\triangle ABC = 3x = 24\sqrt{3}$, E. Wow!!!!

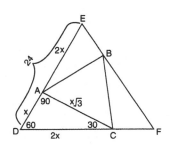

**EXAMPLE 21—**

If a were exactly 6, b would be 8— a 6, 8, 10 Pythagorean triple. Since a is less than 6, b must be greater than 8. It also must be less than the hypotenuse, which is 10. The answer is D. Verrry tricky!

I'm tired of these problems. Let's do something else. Pleeeeze!!!!!

## CHAPTER 16

# VOLUMES, SURFACE AREA, DISTANCE, DISTANCE BETWEEN POINTS

For the SAT, it is necessary to know the surface area and volume of a box and a cube. Actually, we need to know a little more, but we'll look at this later.

## BOX

l = length; w = width; h = height

$V = l \times w \times h$

$SA = 2l \times w + 2w \times h + 2l \times h$

     bottom  sides     front

     + top            + back

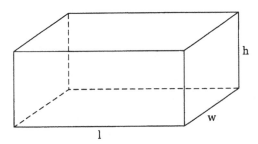

**NOTE:** The only formula you might not want to remember is the surface area of a box. It is sometimes easier to look at the figure and add up the area of the rectangles you see.

**EXAMPLE I—**

$V = 10 \times 5 \times 4 = 200$ cubic feet

$SA = 2(10 \times 4) + 2(5 \times 4) + 2(10 \times 5) = 220$ square feet

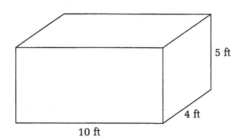

5 ft

4 ft

10 ft

## CUBE

At certain times, the SAT loves the cube. You should know it well!!!!

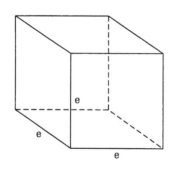

e = edge.

$V = e \times e \times e = e^3$. (Cubing comes from a cube?!! Logical, isn't it?!)

$SA = 6e^2$.

There are 12 edges.

There are 8 vertices.

There are 6 faces (surfaces).

Diagonal in a face. Length $= e\sqrt{2}$.

Diagonal of the cube (one corner on top to opposite corner on bottom). $e\sqrt{3}$.

3-D Pythagorean theorem:

$a^2 + b^2 + c^2 = d^2 \qquad d^2 = e^2 + e^2 + e^2 = 3e^2$

Sooo $d = e\sqrt{3}$.

**EXAMPLE 2—**

$V = 10^3 = 1000$ cubic feet

$SA = 6(10^2) = 600$ square feet

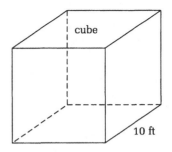

# POINTS ON A GRAPH

Now let's talk about points on a graph. Normally,

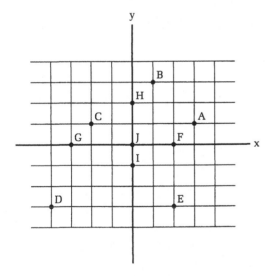

graphing points is about as easy a topic as there is. But the SAT sometimes makes the questions kind of tricky.

First, you must know how to locate points.

A(3,1) B(1,3) Notice order makes a difference.

C(−2,1) D(−4,−3) E(2,−3).

G(−3,0) F(2,0) For any point on x axis, y coordinate is 0!

I(0,−1) H(0,2) For any point on y axis, x coordinate is 0!

J(0,0) Origin.

If the SAT stuck to questions like this, most would be very easy. But. . . .

The graph is divided into four regions called *quadrants*.

> In quadrant I, both x and y are positive. See points A and B in the graph on p. 121.
>
> In quadrant II, y is positive but x is negative. See point C.
>
> In quadrant III, both x and y are negative. See point D.
>
> In quadrant IV, x is positive but y is negative. See point E.
>
> F, G, H, I, J are on the axes and are not in a quadrant.

| | |
|---|---|
| II | I |
| III | IV |

There is a little more you must know.

## Relative Size of x and y

This is something the SAT asks.

> In the shaded area, the y coordinate is bigger than the x coordinate.
>
> In the nonshaded area, the x coordinate is bigger than the y coordinate.

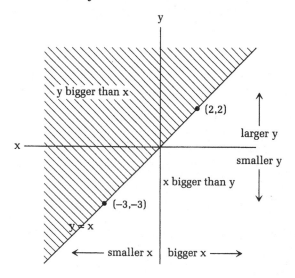

x is sometimes called the *first coordinate*. Guess what y is called.

On the line y = x, the x and y values are equal.

The higher the point, the higher the y value.

The righter the x, the higher the x value.

You may think all of this is silly, but sometimes it gets tricky. Here's a little more.

Horizontal lines are y = something.

x axis, a horizontal line, is y = 0.

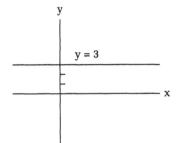

Vertical lines are x = something.

y axis, a vertical line, is x = 0.

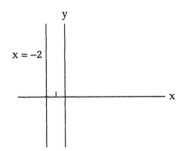

## One-Dimensional Distances

Because the y values are the same, the length of the line segment is the right x minus the left x, 7 − 2 = 5.

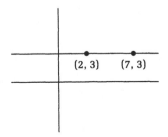

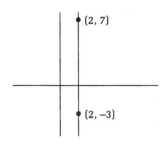

Because the x values are the same, the length of the line segment is top y value minus bottom y value, $7 - (-3) = 10$.

## Two-Dimensional Distance Formula— Old Pythag Again

$$d = \sqrt{(x_2 - x_1)^2 + (y_2 - y_1)^2}$$

Find the distance between $(4, -2)$ and $(9, 5)$

$$d = \sqrt{(9 - 4)^2 + (5 - (-2))^2} = \sqrt{74}$$

## Symmetry

If the point $(x, y)$ is in I, then

$(-x, y)$ is in II

$(-x, -y)$ is in III

$(x, -y)$ is in IV

**NOTE:   We have been using these notations throughout the book.**

The SAT has decided to use four new notations.

1.   Line AB, notation $\overleftrightarrow{AB}$: This picture is here:

2.   Ray AB, with A as the endpoint, notation $\overrightarrow{AB}$. This picture is here:

3.   Line segment AB, notation $\overline{AB}$. The picture is here:

It can be used if the SAT wants you to find the distance between A and B.

4.   The term congruent, notation $\cong$ equal in every way, will now be used.

# LET'S FINALLY TRY SOME PROBLEMS

**EXAMPLE 1—**

(c, d) and (a, b) are equidistant from the
y axis.

a + b + c + d =

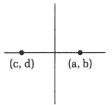

**EXAMPLE 2—**

How many cubes, 2 inches on each side, can be put in
this box?

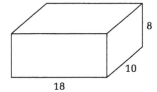

**EXAMPLE 3—**

ABCD is a square. Its area is what?

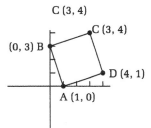

**EXAMPLE 4—**

The box is divided into cubes 10 inches on each
edge. Find the volume of the box.

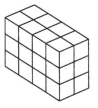

**EXAMPLE 5—**

Box G: volume 20. Box H: volume 40.

A. area of base of G     B. area of base of H
C. area of front of G       D. area of the front of H
E. can't tell

# LET'S LOOK AT THESE ANSWERS

**EXAMPLE 1—**

$d = b = 0$

$a = -c$

Sooo $a + b + c + d = 0$.

**EXAMPLE 2—**

The volume of a $2 \times 2 \times 2$ cube is 8. Annnnd $18 \times 10 \times 8$ divided by 8 (8s cancel) is $18 \times 10 = 180$.

Orrr $\dfrac{18}{2} \times \dfrac{10}{2} \times \dfrac{8}{2} = 9 \times 5 \times 4 = 180$.

**EXAMPLE 3—**

The length of one side is $\sqrt{(1 - 0)^2 + (0 - 3)^2} = \sqrt{10}$.

$s^2 = (\sqrt{10})^2 = 10$. Any two consecutive vertices could be used to find s.

**EXAMPLE 4—**

This is almost Example 2. 2 cubes by 3 cubes by 4 cubes means . . . the dimensions are $20 \times 30 \times 40 = 24{,}000$ cubic units.

**EXAMPLE 5—**

This is a question where, if you look really quickly, you will miss it. The answer is E. The base could be anything in either, for example . . .

Box G: The dimensions could be
$1 \times 1 \times 20$.  Area of the base is 1.  orrrr

$5 \times 4 \times 1$.  Area of the base is 20.

Box H: The dimensions could be
$1 \times 1 \times 30$.  Area of the base is 1.  orrrr
$5 \times 2 \times 3$.  Area of the base is 10.  orrrr
$6 \times 5 \times 1$.  Area of base is 30.

# NEXXXXT . . .

### EXAMPLE 6—

A circle is tangent (just touching) the y axis and has center (–5, –7). Its radius is

A. –5    B. 5    C. –7    D. 7    E. $\sqrt{74}$

### EXAMPLE 7—

L is the line y = x. c – d could equal

A. 10    B. 5    C. 1    D. 0    E. –4000

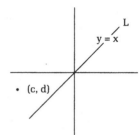

### EXAMPLE 8—

Surface area of the box is what?

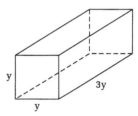

### EXAMPLE 9—

A cube has edge 4. Find the length of the line segment from the middle of one face to a vertex of the opposite face.

### EXAMPLE 10—

The length of $\overline{MN}$ is what?

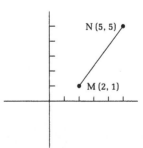

# LET'S LOOK AT HOW TO DO THESE

### EXAMPLE 6—

You must draw a picture and see the radius is 5.
The answer is B. Lengths can't be negative.

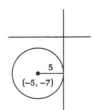

**EXAMPLE 7—**

In the region of (c, d), we know the y value is bigger. The answer is E.

**EXAMPLE 8—**

This is a straight surface area problem. Two squares at the end: Area is $2y^2$. Other 4 sides, $3y^2$: Area is $12y^2$, total $14y^2$.

**EXAMPLE 9—**

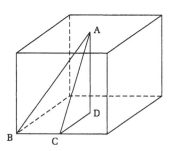

Pretty tough one. If the edge is 4, $\overline{AD}$ is also 4. $\overline{CD}$ is ½ of 4 = 2.

$\overline{AC}^2 = \overline{AD}^2 + \overline{CD}^2 \qquad \overline{AC}^2 = 2^2 + 4^2 = 20 \qquad \overline{BC} \text{ also} = 2$

$\overline{AB}^2 = \overline{BC}^2 + \overline{AC}^2 = 4 + 20 \qquad \overline{AB} = \sqrt{24}$

**EXAMPLE 10—**

Straight distance formula:

$$\sqrt{(5-1)^2 + (4-1)^2} = \sqrt{25} = 5$$

# LET'S TRY FIVE MORE

**EXAMPLE 11—**

The lengths of all sides of a rectangular solid are integers. If the volume is 17, find the area of all of its surfaces.

**EXAMPLE 12—**

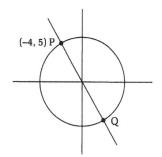

The coordinates of Q are what?

**EXAMPLE 13—**

A cube has a volume of 72 cubic zrikniks. It is divided into 8 ≅ cubes. Find the ratio of the edge of the new cube to the edge of the old cube.

**EXAMPLE 14—**

If the distance from (3, x) to (7, 0) is 5, x may be

A. 0    B. 1    C. 2    D. 3    E. 4

**EXAMPLE 15—**

Area of triangle OCB is what?

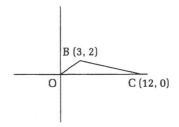

# LET'S ANSWER THESE FIVE

**EXAMPLE 11—**

It doesn't say distinct integers. The only possibility is
1 by 1 by 17.

Two ends are 1 by 1 squares. The total area is 2.

Four others are 1 by 17 rectangles. $17 \times 4 = 68$;
$68 + 2 = 70$.

**EXAMPLE 12—**

By symmetry, Q must be (4, −5).

**EXAMPLE 13—**

We don't care about the measurements or the planet it
is located in. The ratio of

$$v_1/v_2 = e_1^3/e_2^3 = 1/8$$

So $e_1/e_2 = 1/2$.

Notice, we don't need to know what either edge is, just
the ratio.

**EXAMPLE 14—**

$(7 − 3)^2 + (0 − x)^2 = 25$. $x^2 + 16 = 25$. $x^2 = 9$. x could
be 3.      The answer is D.

Trial and error will work also.

**EXAMPLE 15—**

Base of triangle is 12. Height of triangle is 2, the y value of (3, 2). (You should see it.)

$A = \frac{1}{2} \times 2 \times 12 = 12$.

# NEXT FIVE ARE . . .

**EXAMPLE 16—**

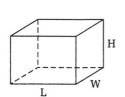

Point Q has coordinates (a, b). If $m > a > b > n$, which points could have coordinates (m, n)?

A. V    B. W    C. X    D. Y    E. Z

**EXAMPLE 17—**

L, W, and H are dimensions of a rectangular box, and all measurements are distinct integers greater than 1. The volume could be

A. 8    B. 12    C. 24    D. 27    E. 98

**EXAMPLE 18—**

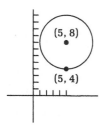

Quadrants satisfying $x/y = 3$.

A. I only    B. I and II    C. I and III    D. II and IV
E. All of them

**EXAMPLE 19—**

Circumference of this circle is what?

**EXAMPLE 20—**

$\dfrac{b}{a} - \dfrac{d}{c}$ is

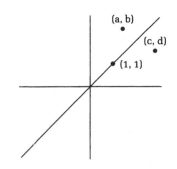

A. always positive
B. always negative
C. sometimes positive
D. sometimes negative
E. sometimes zero

# LET'S LOOK AT THESE ANSWERS

Remember, geometry is a pretty big part of the SAT.

**EXAMPLE 16—**

m > a could be X, Y, or Z, a bigger x value.

b > n could only be X, a smaller y value.      The answer is C.

**EXAMPLE 17—**

The only possibility of 3 distinct factors (not necessarily primes because it doesn't say primes) is $24 = 2 \times 3 \times 4$.      The answer is C.

**EXAMPLE 18—**

The number 3 is misleading. x/y = positive, which means either x and y are both positive or x and y are both negative. I and III.      The answer is C.

**EXAMPLE 19—**

Radius is $8 - 4 = 4$. $c = 2\pi r = 2\pi(4) = 8\pi$.

**EXAMPLE 20—**

All numbers are positive.

In the upper left, y is bigger than x. $b/a > 1$.

In the lower right, x is bigger than y. $d/c < 1$.

Soooo $\dfrac{b}{a} - \dfrac{d}{c}$ is always positive. The answer is A.

## LET'S DO A FINAL FIVE

These are the last five in this section.

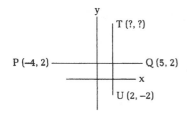

### EXAMPLE 21

$\overline{PQ} = \overline{TU}$ (a little rhyme), and $\overline{PQ}$ is perpendicular to $\overline{TU}$. The point T is

A. (2, 6)    B. (2, 7)    C. (2, 8)    D. (7, 2)    E. (8, 2)

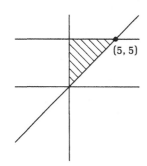

### EXAMPLE 22

Which point is in the shaded area?

A. (2, 4)    B. (–2, 4)    C. (2, 6)    D. (4, 2)    E. (6, 2)

### EXAMPLE 23

Find the volume of a cube if the surface area is $54a^2$ square units.

A. $9a^2$    B. $27a^3$    C. $81a^2$    D. $81a^3$    E. $729a^3$

### EXAMPLE 24

Find the ratio of the volume of a cube with edge $\sqrt{2}$ to the volume of a cube with edge $\sqrt[3]{2}$.

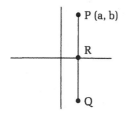

### EXAMPLE 25

The coordinates of Q are

A. (a, –b)    B. (b, a)    C. (b, –a)    D. (–a, b)
E. (–a, –b)

# THE ANSWERS TO THE LAST FIVE ARE . . .

### EXAMPLE 21—

PQ. The y values are the same. The length of the line is the difference in the x's. $5 - (-4) = 9$. $\overline{TU} = \overline{PQ}$ and perpendicular. The perpendicular parts mean the x numbers are the same $(2, ?)$. The equal part means the length of the lines are the same. The y number of T is 9 more than $-2$, which is 7. The answer is. . . . BBBB.

### EXAMPLE 22—

The shaded area has x and y $< 5$, annnnd y is bigger than x, annnnd both coordinates are nonnegative. A is the answer.

### EXAMPLE 23—

$$SA = 6x^2 = 54a^2$$

$$x^2 = 9a^2$$

$$x = 3a$$

$$V = x^3 = (3a)^3 = 27a^3$$

The answer is B.

### EXAMPLE 24—

Ratio of volumes is $(\sqrt{2})^3/(\sqrt[3]{2})^3 = 2\sqrt{2}/2 = \sqrt{2}$.

### EXAMPLE 25—

Vertical lines have the same x values. y is negative. $(a, -b)$. The answer is A.

As much as I would like more, I think it's time to go on to ratios.

## CHAPTER 17

# THE RATIO IS . . .

Hi. I've just taken a mini-, minibreak from the geometry section. The section on ratios overlaps many other topics from the past, as do a number of others. We have already talked about ratio and proportion, which is two ratios equal to each other. What really is a ratio? It is simply a comparison of two items. How do we represent ratios? There are two ways: a new fashion (relatively) and an old fashion.

**EXAMPLE 1—**

Write the ratio of 2 to 5.

"New" way: as a fraction, 2/5

Old way: with a colon, 2:5

**EXAMPLE 2—**

Find the ratio of 5 inches to 2 feet. Answer, 5/24.

The measurements must be the same, and 12 inches = 1 foot, as I hope you know.

**EXAMPLE 3—**

If 20 items cost 46¢, how much do 30 items cost?

$$\frac{\text{cost}}{\text{item}} = \frac{\text{cost}}{\text{item}} \qquad \frac{46}{20} = \frac{x}{30}$$

Cross multiply:

$20x = 46(30)$

Soooo $x = 46(30/20) = 69$.

Even with a calculator, this takes too much time. So we can use a trick. Both 20 and 30 are multiples of 10.

20 cost 46¢

10 cost 23¢      (divide by 2)

30 cost 69¢      (multiply by 3)

I love this stuff. By the way, hopefully you can do this in your head. Remember, you don't want to write anything if possible.

With some problems, you don't even need to know what you are talking about. Let's do one.

## PROBLEMS

**EXAMPLE 4—**

If 5 brigs equal 7 grigs, how many brigs = 11 grigs?

$$\frac{\text{brigs}}{\text{grigs}} = \frac{\text{brigs}}{\text{grigs}} \qquad \frac{5}{7} = \frac{x}{11} \qquad x = 5(11)/7 = 55/7$$

Simple. Huh?

## LET'S TRY SOME REAL (REAL???) PROBLEMS

**EXAMPLE 1—**

The cost of 700 items at $1.50 per 100.

**EXAMPLE 2—**

A wire of uniform density and composition weighs 32 pounds. It is cut into 2 pieces. One is 60 feet and 24 pounds. What is the length of the original piece?

**EXAMPLE 3—**

Of 90 students in a class, the ratio of boys to girls is 2:3. How many girls are in the class?

**EXAMPLE 4—**

Five oranges cost c cents. How many can be bought for y dollars?

**EXAMPLE 5—**

If x is k% of y, what % of y is kx?

**EXAMPLE 6—**

In a certain garden, 1/5 of the flowering plants represent 1/10 of all the flowering plants. What is the ratio of flowering plants to nonflowering plants?

**EXAMPLE 7—**

A jar contains blue and red marbles, 20 in all. Each of the following can be the ratio of blue to red <u>except</u>

A. 1:1     B. 3:2     C. 4:1     D. 5:1     E. 9:1

## LET'S SOLVE THESE

**EXAMPLE 1—**

A simple ratio problem that can be done without ratio.

700/100 = 7 times the amount. 7 × $1.50 = $10.50.

**EXAMPLE 2—**

Ratio trick, trick, trick, trick!!!! Both 32 and 24 are multiples of 8. So

60 feet = 24 pounds

20 feet = 8 pounds     (divide by 3)

80 feet = 32 pounds     (multiply by 4 orrrr add the two together)

### EXAMPLE 3—

Easiest way is $2x + 3x = 90$. $2x$ = boys and $3x$ = girls. $5x = 90$. $x = 18$. $3x = 3(18) = 54$ girls.

### EXAMPLE 4—

$$\frac{\text{cost}}{\text{orange}} = \frac{\text{cost}}{\text{orange}}$$     y dollars = 100y cents

$$\frac{c}{5} = \frac{100y}{?} \qquad ? = 500y/c$$

### EXAMPLE 5—

$$x = \frac{k}{100}\, y \qquad x = \frac{ky}{100} \qquad kx = k\,\frac{ky}{100} = \frac{k^2}{100}\, y$$

$k^2$ percent

### EXAMPLE 6—

1/5 flowering     1/10 total

1 flowering     5/10 total (½ total)

½ flowering and ½ not flowering. Ratio is 1/1!!!! Careful!!!!

### EXAMPLE 7—

1:1 OK (10 and 10); 3:2 OK (12 and 8); 4:1 possible (16 and 4); 9:1 OK (18 to 2). But D is not possible because 5:1 (5 + 1 = 6) is no good since 20 is not a multiple of 6.

# LET'S TRY SEVEN MORE

**EXAMPLE 8—**

If 2/3 of the perimeter of an equilateral triangle is 12, the perimeter is

A. 8    B. 16    C. 18    D. 24    E. 36

**EXAMPLE 9—**

On a map, two cities that are 2.4 inches apart are really 12 miles apart. What is the length of a .2-inch straight road?

**EXAMPLE 10—**

Sugar costs m cents per pound. How many pounds can be bought for $6?

**EXAMPLE 11—**

In a 10-pound solution of water and alcohol, the ratio by mass of water to alcohol is 3:2. A 6-pound solution consisting of 2 parts water to 1 part alcohol is added to the 10-pound solution. What fraction of the new solution is alcohol?

**EXAMPLE 12—**

Q and R are two points to the right of A on the number line:

$2\overline{AQ} = 3\overline{AR}$

What is $\overline{RQ}/\overline{AR}$?

**EXAMPLE 13—**

$a^4 = 5$. $a^3 = 2/c$. Write a in terms of c.

**EXAMPLE 14—**

At a certain school, a L (liters) of milk are needed per week per student. At that rate, b L will supply c students for how many weeks?

# LET'S LOOK AT THE ANSWERS

### EXAMPLE 8—

Only an SAT would ask a question like this. But it is not hard. It doesn't matter that it's an equilateral triangle. $2/3 \, p = 12$. $1/3 \, p = 6$. $p = 18$. Hopefully done in your head.

### EXAMPLE 9—

$.2/.24 = 1/12$ of $12 = 1$.

### EXAMPLE 10—

Same as an earlier one:

$$\frac{m}{1} = \frac{600 \ (\text{cents})}{?} \qquad ? = 600/m \text{ pounds}$$

### EXAMPLE 11—

10 lb 3:2 water      6 lb water      4 lb alcohol

6 lb 2:1 water   $\dfrac{4 \text{ lb water}}{10 \text{ lb water}} \quad \dfrac{2 \text{ lb alcohol}}{6 \text{ lb alcohol}}$   16 lb total

$6/16 = 3/8$ alcohol

A        R        Q

**REASON:** $2 \times 3 = 3 \times 2$

### EXAMPLE 12—

$2\overline{AQ} = 3\overline{AR}$. Let Q be 3 units from A and R 2 units from A as shown in the figure. Clearly, the figure shows $\overline{RQ}/\overline{AR} = 1/2$.

### EXAMPLE 13—

$$\frac{a^4}{a^3} = \frac{5}{2/c}$$

Neat trick. $a = 5c/2$.

**EXAMPLE 14—**

I think this is a toughie. We'll work it with both numbers and letters. Suppose a = 6 L for 1 student for 1 week. Two students for 1 week would be 12. Or, 1 student for 3 weeks would be 18 L. So, if you multiply or divide the students or weeks, leaving the other alone, you would multiply (divide) the liters by the same number. Let c = students = 7. b = 84.

| Liters | Students | Weeks | Liters | Students | Weeks |
|--------|----------|-------|--------|----------|-------|
| 6 | 1 | 1 | a | 1 | 1 |
| 42 | 7 | 1 | ac | c | 1 |
| 1 | 7 | 1/42 | ac/ac = 1 | c | 1/ac |
| 84 | 7 | (1/42)84 | 1(b) = b | c | b(1/ac) = b/ac |
|  |  |  |  |  | is the answer |

This is a particularly tough one, but most ratio problems aren't.

## LET'S DO A FINAL SEVEN

**EXAMPLE 15—**

A gas tank on a tractor holds 18 gallons. A tractor needs 7 gallons to plow 3 acres. How many acres does the tractor plow with a full gas tank?

**EXAMPLE 16—**

A penguin swims at 8 m/s (meters per second). How long does it take the penguin to swim 100 m?

**EXAMPLE 17—**

If z is 70% of y, and x is 60% of y, the ratio of z to x is what?

**EXAMPLE 18—**

It takes 10 people 12 hours to do a job. How many hours will it take for 6 people to do ¼ of the job?

**EXAMPLE 19—**

$$\frac{b+a}{b} = 2 \qquad \frac{c+a}{a} = 3 \qquad b/c = ?$$

**EXAMPLE 20—**

The ratio of Sandy's salary to Chris's salary is 2 to 5. The ratio of Sandy's salary to Cory's salary is 7 to 9. Find the ratio of Chris's salary to Cory's.

**EXAMPLE 21—**

What is the thickness of 1 sheet of paper if 500 sheets is 2.5 inches thick?

## LET'S LOOK AT THE LAST SEVEN ANSWERS

**EXAMPLE 15—**

Straight proportion. $7/3 = 18/a$. Acres $a = 54/7$ acres.

**EXAMPLE 16—**

SAT distance problem up to this point. Up to this point in time, this is how the SAT has asked distance problems. Rate $\times$ time = distance. Soooo, distance over rate = time. $100/8 = 12.5$ seconds.

**EXAMPLE 17—**

$z = .7y$

Divide!!!!    $\dfrac{z}{x} = \dfrac{.7}{.6} = 7/6$    That's it.

$x = .6y$

**EXAMPLE 18—**

You have to look at it as 120 hours to finish one job; 30 hours for ¼ of the job. Six people would take 5 hours to finish ¼ of the job. $(6)(5) = 30$.

**EXAMPLE 19—**

$$\frac{b+a}{b} = \frac{b}{b} + \frac{a}{b} = 2 \qquad \text{So } \frac{a}{b} = 1$$

$$\frac{c+a}{a} = \frac{c}{a} + \frac{a}{a} = 3 \qquad \text{So } \frac{c}{a} = 2$$

$$\frac{a}{b} \times \frac{c}{a} = \frac{c}{b} = 2 \times 1 = 2 \qquad \frac{b}{c} = 1/2$$

**EXAMPLE 20—**

Similar problem.

$$\frac{S}{Ch} = \frac{2}{5} \qquad \frac{S}{Co} = \frac{7}{9}$$

$$\frac{Ch}{Co} = \frac{Ch}{S} \frac{S}{Co} = \frac{5}{2} \times \frac{7}{9} = \frac{35}{18}$$

There are other ways, such as Example 17.

**EXAMPLE 21—**

Simple ratio, but the larger number is on the bottom:

$$\frac{2.5}{500} = \frac{5}{1000} = .005$$

Let us take a look at the trends of the SAT since 1993. We have already mentioned the increase in algebra, especially exponents. So far I think there are four trends: Two I think are kind of easy; a third I think will rarely come up, and a fourth. Let's look, comparing them to what has come before.

## CHAPTER 18

# CHANGES, AROUND THE YEAR 1993

## CYLINDERS

The SAT has added the formula of the volume of a cylinder to the list of formulas you need to know. I have seen more than 60 past SAT and PSAT exams. On none of them did you need to know the formula.

I have a crazy head. I can make up SATs. But to this point I find it very difficult to make up questions about the volume of the cylinder. The SAT has had a few, but they are indeed strange. I suspect these kinds of questions will be few and far between. Of course, at most one will appear on any SAT. I don't think you should worry about it. Let me give you the formula, a straightforward question, and an SAT-type one.

Volume = $\pi r^2 h$
r = radius of the circular base and h = height

## PROBLEMS

**EXAMPLE 1—**

Find the volume of a cylinder if the diameter of the base and the height are both 6.

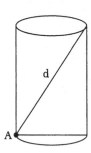

### EXAMPLE 2—

The radius of the base of a cylinder is 4. From a point farthest from point A on the base is another point. If the height is 6, find the distance to that point.

## SOLUTIONS

### EXAMPLE I—

$$d = 6 \qquad r = 3 \qquad V = \pi r^2 h = V = \pi(3)^2 6 = 54\pi$$

### EXAMPLE 2—

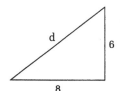

If you look at the picture, we have a simple Pythag triple, 6, 8, . . . 10!!

## SLOPE

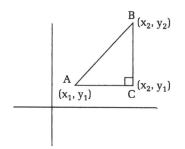

The slope of a line has been indirectly talked about before. It seems to be more in the consciousness of those who make up the SAT. Let us define slope formally:

$$\text{Slope } m = \frac{y_2 - y_1}{x_2 - x_1} = \frac{\text{change in } y}{\text{change in } x}$$

### EXAMPLE I—

   a. Find the slope between (2, 3) and (5, 7).

   b. Find the slope between (3, −4) and (−1, 1).

   c. Find the slope between (1, 5) and (4, 5).

   d. Find the slope between (2, 2) and (2, 6).

If you walk from left to right and you get to the line and you go up, the slope is POSITIVE, like 1(a).

If you go left to right and the line is at your head, this
is a NEGATIVE slope, like 1(b).

$$1b.\ m = \frac{1 - (-4)}{-1 - 3} = \frac{5}{-4}$$

$$1a.\ m = \frac{7 - 3}{5 - 2} = \frac{4}{3}$$

$$= -\frac{5}{4} = \frac{-5}{4}$$

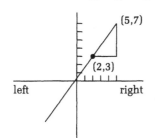

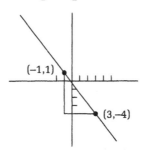

Horizontal lines have ZERO slope 1(c).
Vertical lines have NO SLOPE or the slope is said to be
UNDEFINED 1(d).

$$1c.\ \frac{5 - 5}{4 - 1} = 0/3 = 0 \qquad 1d.\ \frac{6 - 2}{2 - 2} = \frac{4}{0}\ \text{undefined}$$

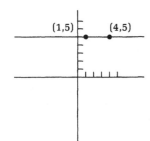

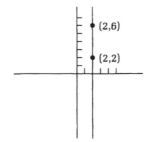

One form of the equation of a line is $y = mx + b$. The
coefficient of x, m, is the slope. The y intercept is
(0,b). If $x = 0$, then $y = b$.

If $y = -2x + 4$, the slope is −2, and the y intercept is
4, the point (0,4).

If $y = x$, the slope is 1 (since $x = 1x$), and the y intercept is the origin (0, 0).

## LET'S DO SOME PROBLEMS. . .

### EXAMPLE 1—

A line is connecting (0, 0) and (12, 16). Another point on this line is

A. (2, 3)    B. (3, 2)    C. (4, 3)    D. (3, 4)    E. (16, 12)

### EXAMPLE 2—

If the points (1, 2) and (x, 8) are on a line with the slope 2, x might be

A. 2    B. 3    C. 4    D. 5    E. 6

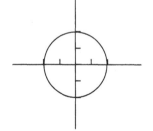

### EXAMPLE 3—

The slope of the line tangent (just touching) the circle at the point (0, 2) is

A. 0    B. 2    C. undefined    D. 1
E. unable to determine the slope

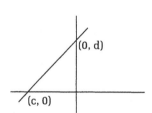

### EXAMPLE 4—

The slope of this line is

A. c/d    B. –c/d    C. d/c    D. –d/c    E. cd

## SOLUTIONS

### EXAMPLE 1—

m between points given is

$$\frac{16 - 0}{12 - 0} = 16/12 = 4/3$$

D also has the same slope with (0, 0).

**EXAMPLE 2—**

$$\frac{8-2}{x-1} = 2/1 \qquad 6 = 2(x-1) \qquad 2x = 8 \qquad x = 4$$

The answer is C.

**EXAMPLE 3—**

Horizontal line. m = 0.

**EXAMPLE 4—**

$$m = \frac{d-0}{0-c} = d/(-c) = D$$

Let's go on.

# EQUATION

After talking about slope, the next logical topic is the equation of the line. The specific equation of the line the SAT talks about is y = mx + b.

If we solve for y, the coefficient of x, m, is the slope.

The letter b is the y intercept. If a line hits the y-axis, x = 0. If x = 0, y = b.

**EXAMPLE I—**

If a line goes through the points (1, 2) and (4, 11), find b.

$$m = \frac{11-2}{4-1} = 3.\ y = mx + b.$$ Choose one point, in this case (1, 2) (easier numbers).

m = 3. Substitute in y = mx + b: m = 3, x = 1, y = 2. We get 2 = 3(1) + b. b = −1.

**EXAMPLE 2—**

If the slope is −3 and the x intercept 4, find the y intercept.

If the y intercept is x = 0, then the x intercept is y = 0. The x intercept is (4, 0).

We have m = −3, x = 4, and y = 0. Substitute: y = mx + b; 0 = (−3)(4) + b. b = 12.

## HERE ARE SOME PROBLEMS

### EXAMPLE 1—

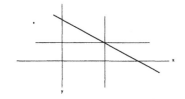

Picture showing the lines x = 4 (and the x intercept) and y = 2 (y intercept).

The slope of the pictured line is −1. The y intercept is what?

A.  2        B.  4        C.  6        D.  8        E.  10

### EXAMPLE 2—

f(3) = 1 and f(2) = 5. The y intercept is what?

A.  1        B.  3        C.  −4        D.  11
E.  13

### EXAMPLE 3—

f(2) = 5 and the y intercept is −11. The slope is what?

## SOLUTIONS

### EXAMPLE 1—

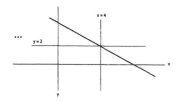

The lines meet at the point (4, 2) or x = 4 and y = 2. m = −1.

Substitute in y = mx + b. 2 = (−1)(4) + b. b = 6. The answer is C.

### EXAMPLE 2

We have points (3, 1) and (2, 5). m = $\dfrac{5 - 1}{2 - 3}$ = −4.

Since m = −4, x = 3, and y = 1, y = m x + b is 1 = (−4)(3) + b. b = 13.      The answer is E.

Notice we could use either point. If we chose (2, 5), x = 2, y = 5, and m = −4.

Then y = mx + b is 5 = (−4) 2 + b.   b is still 13.

**EXAMPLE 3**

f(2) = 5 means x = 2 and y = 5; b = −11.

y = mx + b. 5 = (2)m − 11. 2m = 16; the slope is 8.

# GRAPHS AND CHARTS

The SAT still has its share of charts and graphs. There are the usual ones and the strange ones. To these the SAT seems to have added ones I've seen on the GRE exam (Graduate Record Exam, the one that college seniors take to get into graduate school). These charts concern percentages on charts. We'll do one here and at least one on one of the practice SATs.

# PROBLEMS

**EXAMPLE 1**

We take the sum of numbers x + y, where x is taken from column X and y is taken from column Y. The total number of distinct sums is

A. 4     B. 6     C. 7     D. 8     E. 16

| X | Y |
|---|---|
| 2 | 4 |
| 3 | 5 |
| 4 | 6 |
| 5 | 7 |

**EXAMPLE 2**

$2100 is Sandy's monthly budget. Of the $2100, what is spent on rent?

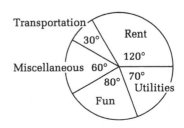

**EXAMPLE 3**

The difference between the % B increased, and the % A increased is what?

Widget Costs of Company A and Company B

## LET'S LOOK AT SOME ANSWERS

**EXAMPLE 1**

It does not matter what makes up the sum. 3 + 5 and 4 + 4 give the same result, 8. There are 7 distinct sums 6, 7, 8, 9, 10, 11, and 12. The answer is C.

**EXAMPLE 2**

120° = 120/360 = 1/3 of the circle. 1/3 of $2100 is $700.

**EXAMPLE 3**

This is a really mild example of percent differences.

*Company A:* The increase is from $800 to $1400, an increase of $600.

*Company B:* The increase is from $400 to $1000, an increase of $600.

We are interested in % increases. % increases are based on the original amount (also % decreases).

*Company A:* $600/$800 = 75%.

*Company B:* $600/$400 = 150%.

150% − 75% = 75%

Sometimes they will give a scatter diagram. For example, suppose there is a survey of 15 brands of cereal. Of the 5 brands labeled, which has the cheapest cost per ounce?

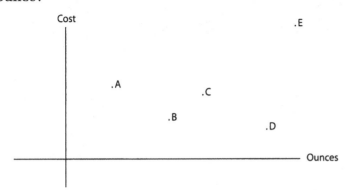

Of the 5 brands the letter D is the cheapest w > t per ounce because the slope of a line through this point and the origin is the smallest positive slope.

## "STORY" WORD PROBLEMS

I have seen about 60 SATs, maybe a few more. Until about 1994, I can remember only one regular "story" word problem. After the change in format, I think I've seen four or five. Therefore, we'll look at the old-time word problems, which are still present, and the new ones. But you should NOT worry about them. I have never seen an SAT with more than one of these. If you get 1 wrong and 59 right, you'll get a pretty good score.

### Age Problems

*The older kind:* Mary was d years old b years ago. How old will she be in c years?

*The newer kind:* John is 4 times the age of Mary. In 5 years he will be 3 times as old as Mary. What are their ages now?

*The older kind solution:* The secret is the age now. b

years ago, Mary's age was d. Now, b years later, her age is d + b. c years in the future? d + b + c. If it were m years ago you were looking for, it would have been d + b − m.

You could also substitute numbers, but this is much quicker.

*The newer kind solution:* A chart will be helpful. On the SAT don't use lines—takes too much time. Let x = smaller number, Mary's age:

|  | Age now | Age in 5 years |
|------|---------|----------------|
| John | 4x | 4x + 5 |
| Mary | x | x + 5 |

In 5 years he will be 3 times as old as Mary

$$4x + 5 = 3(x + 5)$$

$4x + 5 = 3x + 15$. $x = 10$ Mary's age. $4x = 40$ John's age. That's it.

## Coin Problems (Also Ticket Problems)

*Old style:* Find the total amount of money if you have n nickels, d dimes, and q quarters.

*New style:* There are 20 coins in dimes and nickels. The total is $1.70. How many dimes?

Both problems depend on the same things. 7 nickels is 7(5) = 35¢. 8 dimes is 8(10) = 80¢ in value. In other words, the value of a coin (or ticket) times the number of coins (or tickets) is the total $.

*Old style:* Value of n nickels is 5n; d dimes? 10d; q quarters? 25q. Total value is 5n + 10d + 25q.

*New style:*

| | Value of a Coin | × | Number of Coins | = | Total Amount of Money |
|---|---|---|---|---|---|
| nickels | 5 | | 20 − x | | 5(20 − x) |
| dimes | 10 | | x | | 10x |
| totals | | | 20 | | 170 |

5(20 − x) + 10x  = 170

100 −  5x +  10x = 170

   5x          =  70      x = 14 dimes.

Never check on the SAT. Not enough time.

**NOTE 1**

Total money is in pennies.

**NOTE 2**

20 coins. If x is one part, 20 − x is the other. (If one were 6, the other would be 20 − 6.)

## Alcohol Problems

Alcohol problems are the same. We've done the older kind. Oh, well let's do one.

*New:* How many ounces of 40% alcohol must be mixed with 6 ounces of 70% alcohol to give a 50% solution?

If something is 40% alcohol and we have 20 pounds, .40 × 20 = 8 pounds of alcohol. Okay, alcohol doesn't come in pounds, but who cares? You get the idea.

Amount of a solution x% alcohol = amount of alcohol

Since all three (A, B, and Mixture) have %, we can eliminate the decimal point and the problem still works.

| | Amount of Solution | × | Percent Alcohol | = | Amount of Alcohol |
|---|---|---|---|---|---|
| A | x | | 40 | | 40x |
| B | 6 | | 70 | | 420 |
| mixture (total) | x + 6 | | 50 | | 50(x + 6) |

$$40x + 420 = 50(x + 6)$$
$$40x + 420 = 50x + 300$$
$$120 = 10x$$
$$x = 12$$

Pleeeezzzze, do NOT worry too much about these. You should work on getting all the ones you know right. You'll get a good score that way.

## MISCELLANEOUS

This section is the reason it is impossible to teach anyone to get 800. Basically, this section would have to be 500 pages for you to have a chance for 800. But the SAT still asks questions that were never asked before and never will be again. If you can figure them out, and get everything else correct, you might be able to get 800.

## PROBLEMS

### EXAMPLE 1—

There are 8 people in a circle. Each shakes each other's hand once. How many handshakes?

### EXAMPLE 2—

A lunch consists of 1 sandwich, 1 soup, and 1 drink. The choice is from 6 soups, 3 sandwiches, and 2 drinks. How many different meals are possible?

**EXAMPLE 3—**

A bowl has 7 red balls and 5 yellow balls.

    a. One ball is selected. Find the probability the ball is yellow.

    b. Two balls are selected without replacement. Find the probability that both balls are yellow.

    c. Two balls are selected with replacement. Find the probability that both balls are red.

## SOLUTIONS

**EXAMPLE 1—**

There are two ways to look at this.

**METHOD 1**

Person 1 shakes 7 peoples' hands. Person 2 shakes 6 peoples' hands, because 1 person's hand was shaken already.

$7 + 6 + 5 + 4 + 3 + 2 + 1 = 28$

**METHOD 2**

Each person shakes 7 hands. $8 \times 7 = 56$. Buuut each pair is counted twice (person 3 shakes 4 and 4 shakes 3). ½ of 56 = 28.

**EXAMPLE 2—**

The answer is $6 \times 3 \times 2 = 36$. This is called the *principal of counting*. If you can do $a_1$ in m ways, $a_2$ in n ways, $a_3$ in p ways, . . . the total number of ways you can do $a_1$ first, then $a_2$ second, $a_3$ next . . . is $m \times n \times p \times$ . . .

**EXAMPLE 3—**

Probability = total successes over total number. y =

    a. Pr (yellow) = 5/12

b. Pr(y) = 5/12. No replacement Pr (2nd yellow) = 4/11. (1 yellow gone; one ball gone.) Pr (1st yellow, then 2nd yellow) = (5/12)(4/11) = 5/33.

c. Watch. We changed to red. Pr (red, then red, replacement) = (7/12)(7/12) = 49/144.

Notice in b and c we are using Example 2.

## LET'S DO SOME MORE

### EXAMPLE 4—

We have the sequence 1, 2, 3, 4, 5, 1, 2, 3, 4, 5, 1, . . . . The 798th entry is

A. 1    B. 2    C. 3    D. 4    E. 5

### EXAMPLE 5—

Suppose $a * b = b^2 - 5a$.

I.  What is 2 * 10?

II. If $b * b = 6$, what are the values of b?

## SOLUTIONS

### EXAMPLE 4—

This is a different kind of counting problem. Sometimes in mathematics, counting is easy, sometimes it is hard, and sometimes it is tricky. This sequence is cyclic (goes in a cycle). The cycle is 5. Soooo $5\overline{)798}$. We don't care about the answer. The remainder is 3. The answer is C.

### EXAMPLE 5—

The SAT used to love, love, love this kind of problem. Now it only loves them.

It is a made-up operation. Your job is to follow directions.

I.  $a * b = b^2 - 5a$. These directions tell you to square

the number after the * and subtract 5 times the number before the * sign:

$$2 * 10 = 10^2 - 5(2) = 100 - 10 = 90$$

II.  $b * b = b^2 - 5b = 6$. So $b^2 - 5b - 6 = 0$.

$$(b - 6)(b + 1) = 0 \qquad b = 6 \qquad \text{and} \qquad b = -1.$$

**NOTE**

Many, many, many, many symbols are used beside the *.

## CHAPTER 19

# CHANGES FOR THE TWENTY-FIRST CENTURY

## A. ALGEBRAIC EQUATIONS

I believe one reason this section has been added to the SAT is that too many high school textbooks neglect these topics!!!

### Equations with More than One Letter

A. *Sometimes an equation has **two letters**.* We want to be able to solve them.

**EXAMPLE 1—**

Solve for x: $\dfrac{ax}{a + x} = \dfrac{2}{3}$.

*Answer:* If an equation has two letters, almost always the solution is to cross multiply.

| | |
|---|---|
| $3ax = 2(a + x)$ | Cross multiply. |
| $3ax = 2a + 2x$ | Distributive law. |
| $3ax - 2x = 2a$ | Get all the terms with x on the left. |

$$x(3a - 2) = 2a \qquad \text{Take the common x factor out!}$$

$$x = \frac{2a}{3a - 2} \qquad \text{Divide by } 3a - 2.$$

**B.** *Solve for x with only **one letter** and fractions.* The SAT seems to want to emphasize this area more. Let's do three problems.

**EXAMPLE 1—**

Solve for x: $\dfrac{x - 3}{x - 5} = \dfrac{5}{3}$.

*Answer:* Like always, we cross multiply:

$5(x - 5) = 3(x - 3)$.   $5x - 25 = 3x - 9$.
$2x = 16$. $x = 8$.

**EXAMPLE 2—**

Solve for x: $\dfrac{x - 2}{x - 4} = \dfrac{x + 1}{x + 3}$.

*Answer:* Again, we cross multiply:

$(x - 4)(x + 1) = (x - 2)(x + 3)$.   $x^2 - 3x - 4$
$= x^2 + x - 6$.

The x squares cancel: $-4x = -2$.   $x = -2/-4 = 1/2$.

**NOTE**

If the answer were either 4 or $-3$, there would be no answer to the problem since the denominator can nevvvvver equal zero!

**EXAMPLE 3—**

Solve for x: $\dfrac{x - 6}{x^2} = \dfrac{1}{3}$.

*Answer:* Again we cross multiply. Buuut, x squared does not disappear. So we have to factor:

$x^2 (1) = 3(x + 6).$   $x^2 = 3x + 18.$   $x^2 - 3x - 18 = 0.$

$(x - 6)(x + 3) = 0.$   $x - 6 = 0$ and $x + 3 = 0.$   Sooo, $x = 6$ and $x = -3.$

**C.** *Sometimes an equation has **absolute value**.* If $|x| = 6$, x has two answers, $+6$ and $-6$.

If $|x| = 0$, then the only answer is $x = 0$.

If $|x| = -3$, then there is no answer to the equation because the absolute value is nevvver negative.

**EXAMPLE 1—**

$|x - 4| = 6$

*Answer:* This means $x - 4 = 6$ or $x - 4 = -6$.   Sooo, $x = 10$ and $-2$.

**EXAMPLE 2—**

$|2x + 3| = 0$

*Answer:* This means $2x + 3 = 0$.   Solving $x = -3/2$.

**EXAMPLE 3—**

$|5x - 7| = -2$

*Answer:* This has no solution because the absolute value is never negative.

# LET'S TRY SOME PROBLEMS

**PROBLEM 1—**

$\dfrac{cx}{d - x} = 1.$   $x =$

A.  d/c     B.  d/2c     C.  d/(c − 1)     D.  d/(c + 1)
E.  (c − 1)/d

**PROBLEM 2—**

$y = \dfrac{x - 3}{x + 4}.$   x in terms of y is what?

**PROBLEM 3—**

  x y = x + y has no solutions if x =

A. −2   B. x = −1   C. x = 0   D. x = 1
E. x = 2

**PROBLEM 4—**

The solution set of | 3x − 5 | = 2 is

A. x = 7 and x = 3   B. x = 1 and x = 7/3
C.  x = 3 only   D. x = 7/3 only   E. x = 1 only

**PROBLEM 5—**

x is an integer and | x | = x

A.  only for x = 0.
B.  if x is all integers.
C.  if x is all nonnegative integers.
D.  if x is any odd integer.
E.  if x is any even integer.

**PROBLEM 6—**

$\dfrac{x}{4} = \dfrac{9}{x}.$   x =?

# SOLUTIONS

**PROBLEM 1—**

$\dfrac{cx}{d - x} = 1$

Sooo, cx = d − x.   cx + x = d.   x(c + 1) = d, and
x = d/(c + 1).

The answer is D.

**PROBLEM 2—**

$\dfrac{y}{1} = \dfrac{x+3}{x-4}.$   In an equation on the SAT, alllways cross

multiply.

$y(x-4) = x+3.$   $xy-4y = x+3.$   $xy-x = 4y+3.$   $x(y-1) = 4y+3.$

$x = (4y+3)/(y-1).$ Of course, on the SAT this will be a multiple-choice question.

**PROBLEM 3—**

This actually can be done two ways:

**First,** you can substitute each number in the equation. You don't have to solve.

You only have to see there is a solution.

$x = -2$: $2y = -2 + y$ has a solution;

$x = -1$: $-y = -1 + y$ has a solution;

$x = 0$: $y = 0$ has a solution;

$x = 1$: $y = 1 + y$ has no solution since you can't add 1 to a number and get the same answer.

**Second,** you can solve for y:  $xy = x + y$; $xy - y = x$; $y(x-1) = x.$

$y = x/(x-1)$ has no solution for $x = 1$ since the denominator can't be zero.

[See the section on functions (domain and range).]

**PROBLEM 4—**

$3x - 5 = 2$ or $3x - 5 = -2$; $x = 7/3$ or 1; the answer is B.

**PROBLEM 5—**

The answer is C.

**PROBLEM 6—**

Cross multiply: $x^2 = 36$. $x = \pm\sqrt{36} = \pm 6$.

**D.** *Sometimes equations will have a **square root** in them.* I will show you how to solve them. However, most of the time it is better just to substitute in the choices.

**EXAMPLE 1—**

Solve for x: $2\sqrt{x} + 7 = 13$.

*Answer:* $2\sqrt{x} = 6$ — Subtract 7 from both sides.

$\sqrt{x} = 3$ — Divide both sides by 2.

$x = 9$ — Square both sides.

This one's not too bad to solve. However, . . .

**EXAMPLE 2—**

$\sqrt{2x - 4} + \sqrt{x} = 4$

*Answer:*

$\sqrt{2x - 4} = 4 - \sqrt{x}$. — Isolate the messier square root.

$2x - 4 = 16 - 8\sqrt{x} + x$. — Square both sides.

$8\sqrt{x} = -x + 20$. — Collect like terms and again isolate the remaining square root.

$64x = x^2 - 40x + 400$. — Again square both sides.

$0 = x^2 - 104x + 400$. — Again collect like terms on one side.

$0 = (x - 100)(x - 4)$. $x = 4, 100$. — Factor. Set each factor $= 0$ and solve.

$x = 4$ is the answer since it is the only one that checks in the original equation.

The SAT will give problems that are shorter than this one. Trial and error for many of these will be the shortest way to solve them.

## LET'S TRY SOME PRACTICE

**PROBLEM 1—**

$\sqrt{x-1} = x - 1$ is true for x =

A. 0    B. 1    C. 2    D. 1 and 2    E. 0, 1, and 2

**PROBLEM 2—**

If $3\sqrt{x} = -3\sqrt{x}$, x =

A. 0    B. 1    C. 100    D. 10,000
E. all real numbers

## SOLUTIONS

**PROBLEM 1—**
The answer is D.

**PROBLEM 2—**
The answer is A. Remember, $\sqrt{1}$ = only 1,
*not* 1 and − 1.

More on these topics? See *Algebra for the Clueless* and *Precalc with Trig for the Clueless.*

### Inequalities

Let's look at inequalities.

*We solve linear inequalities in exactly the same way we solve equalities except if we multiply or divide each side by negatives, the order reverses.*

**EXAMPLE 1—**

$3 > 2$ buut $3(-2) = -6 < 2(-2) = -4$

since $-4$ is to the right of $-6$ on the number line.

**EXAMPLE 2—**

$12 > -9$ buut $12/-3 = -4 < -9/-3 = 3$.

**EXAMPLE 3—**

Solve for x:

$4x - 3 \geq 6x - 9$

| | |
|---|---|
| *Answer:* $-2x - 3 \geq -9$ | Subtracting 6x from both sides **doesn't** change the order. |
| $-2x \geq -6$ | Adding 3 to each side **doesn't** change the order. |
| $x \leq 3$ | Dividing both sides by $-2$ **changes** the order. |

**EXAMPLE 4—**

$|x| < 4$ means x is between $-4$ and 4 orrrr
$-4 < x < 4$.

**EXAMPLE 5—**

$|2x - 5| < 7$

| | |
|---|---|
| $-7 < 2x - 5 < 7$ | The meaning of this absolute value. |
| $-2 < 2x < 12$ | Adding 5 to each of the three pieces of the inequality. |
| $-1 < x < 6$ | Dividing each piece by 2. |

**EXAMPLE 6—**

$|x| > 4$ means $x > 4$ or $x < -4$ !

**EXAMPLE 7—**

$|x - 7| > 3$

$x - 7 > 3$ or $x - 7 < -3$, the meaning of this absolute value.

So $x > 10$ or $x < 4$     Solving each part separately.

**NOTE 1**

$|x - 5| \geq -3$ is true for all x's because the absolute value, which is never negative, must be always bigger than a negative number. (Zero and all positives are bigger than all negatives.)

**NOTE 2**

$|x - 6| < -2$ has no solution because a positive (or zero) can't be less than a negative.

## Quadratic Inequality

I really don't think the SAT will ask this, but I can't take the chance.

**EXAMPLE 8—**

Solve for x:

$$\frac{5x - 7}{x - 1} \geq 4$$

*Answer:* Unlike equations, if you cross multiply inequalities, you are wrong, wrong wrong!!!!

$$\frac{5x - 7}{x - 1} - \frac{4}{1} \geq 0 \qquad \text{Subtract 4 from each side.}$$

$$\frac{(5x - 7)(1) - 4(x - 1)}{(x - 1)1} \qquad \text{or} \qquad \frac{x - 3}{x - 1} \geq 0 \qquad \text{Subtract}$$

and simplify.

A fraction equals zero if the top is zero and the bottom is zero. $x = 3$, but $x \neq 1$

On the number line put a solid dot on 3 and an open dot on 1.

Substitute a number in each of the regions. You will find the statement is true if $x \geq 3$ or $x < 1$.

## HERE ARE SOME PROBLEMS

**PROBLEM 1—**

When is $x - 3 > 0$ and $x - 6 < 0$?

A. always      B. never      C. $x > 3$
D. $x < 6$      E. $3 < x < 6$

**PROBLEM 2—.**

When is $x - 3 > 0$ or $x - 6 < 0$?

A. always      B. never      C. $x > 3$      D. $x < 6$
E. $6 > x > 3$

**PROBLEM 3—**

When is $|x - 6| < 2$?

A. $x = 8$ and $4$      B. $x < 8$      C. $x > 4$
D. $4 < x < 8$      E. $x < 4$ or $x > 8$

**PROBLEM 4—**

When is $|x - 5| > 0$?

A. always      B. $x = 5$      C. $x \neq 5$      D. $x = 0$
E. $x \neq 0$

**PROBLEM 5—**

When is $\dfrac{(x - 6)}{(x - 3)^2} > 0$?

A. $x > 6$      B. $x \neq 3$      C. $x > 6$ or $x < 3$
D. $x < 3$      E. always

## SOLUTIONS

**PROBLEM 1—**

"And" means at the same time; $x - 3 > 0$ means $x > 3$;
$x - 6 < 0$ means $x < 6$.
At the same time?     The answer is E.

**PROBLEM 2**

"Or" means one or the other or both. Every number is covered at least once.     The answer is A.

**PROBLEM 3**

Here is another way to do the problem. Set $|x - 6| = 2$. Better, in your head or write down $x - 6 = 2$ or $x - 6 = -2$. $x = 8$ and 4. Because it is less than, $<$, the answer is the middle, $4 < x < 8$, D. If it had been greater than, the answer would have been E, the outsides. Again, the answer here is D.

**PROBLEM 4**

The only time this is not true is when $x - 5 = 0$. $x$ can't equal 5, C!

**PROBLEM 5**

$(x - 3)^2$ is alllways $> 0$, except when $x = 3$ (undefined). We only worry about the top.

$x - 6 > 0$ means $x > 6$. The answer is, dah dah, C!

*Precalc with Trig for the Clueless* and *Algebra for the Clueless* are the places to look for more details.

## Complex Fractions

This is a topic the SAT sneaked into the test without anyone noticing. Well, I noticed.

A *complex fraction* is a fraction with other fractions in it. Let us do two.

**EXAMPLE 1**

Simplify $\dfrac{1/6 + 2/3}{2 - 3/4}$.

*Answer:* The LCD of all the fractions is 12.

$$\frac{12/1 \times 1/6 + 12/1 \times 2/3}{12/1 \times 2/1 - 12/1 \times 3/4} = \frac{2 + 8}{24 - 9} = \frac{10}{15} = \frac{2}{3}$$

**EXAMPLE 2—**

Simplify: $\dfrac{1/x^2 - 1/y^2}{1/x - 1/y}$.

*Answer:* The LCD is $x^2y^2$.

$\dfrac{(x^2y^2/1)\,1/x^2 - (x^2y^2/1)\,1/y^2}{(x^2y^2/1)\,1/x - (x^2y^2/1)\,1/y} =$ Multiplying every fraction by the LCD.

$\dfrac{y^2 - x^2}{xy^2 - x^2y} =$    Dividing the fractions. See how much better it looks?

$\dfrac{(y + x)(y - x)}{xy(y - x)} = \dfrac{y + x}{xy}$    Factor top and bottom, and reduce.

Let's try a problem:

Let $q = 1/p$. $\dfrac{1 - p}{1 - q}$ equals

A. 1    B. $(1 - p)$    C. $(p - 1)$    D. p
E. $-p$

*Answer:* We substitute:

$$\frac{1 - p}{1 - q} = \frac{1 - p}{1 - 1/p} = \frac{p(1 - p)}{p(1 - 1/p)} = \frac{p(1 - p)}{(p - 1)} = -1 \times p$$
$$= -p \text{ since } (1 - p)/(p - 1) = -1.$$

The secret of this problem is not to multiply out the numerator.

## B. FUNCTIONS AND FUNCTIONAL NOTATION, AND A LITTLE ON EXPONENTIAL GROWTH

The SAT finally added functions to the SAT. It is the most serious omission from high school. It is better today than it was in the 1960s and 1970s, but it is not what it should be.

Here we will give you enough to do well on the SAT. If you want more, you should see *Algebra for the Clueless*. *Precalc with Trig for the Clueless* is filled with functions for those who really want to know and understand functions. It is one of the keys to higher math skills.

**DEFINITION**

**Function:**  To each element in D, we assign 1 and only 1 value.

**EXAMPLE I—**

We have a function. To the number 1, we assign the letter a. To 2 we assign the number 3. To 3 we assign the number 3. To 4 we assign a pig.

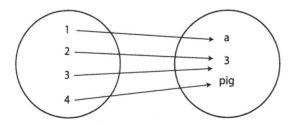

**LOTS OF NOTES**

1.  The set D is called the **domain**. We should think of the x values. D = {1, 2, 3, 4}.

2.  Although it is not part of the definition, there is another set in the problem. We call it the **range**, R. In this case R = {a, 3, pig}. For the range we should think of y values.

3. The domain and range can have the same elements or totally different elements.

4. We can't keep drawing pictures of functions. We need what is called *functional notation*.

**EXAMPLE I REVISITED—**

$f(1) = a$

Read, "f of 1 is a." $f(2) = 3$. $f(3) = 3$. $f(4) = $ pig.

5. Functions are usually given in formula form.

6. The letters f, g, F, and G are the most likely letters that will be used for functions.

**EXAMPLE 2—**

$f(x) = x^2 + 3x + 8$      $D = \{5, 0, -4, \text{pig}\}$

$f(5) = 5^2 + 3(5) + 8 = 48$      $f(0) = 0^2 + 3(0) + 8 = 8$

$f(-4) = (-4)^2 + 3(-4) + 8 = 12$      $f(\text{pig}) = \text{pig}^2 + 3 \text{ pig} + 8$      $R = \{48, 8, 12, \text{pig}^2 + 3 \text{ pig} + 8\}$

This is an example of part of a *parabola*. We will talk a little more of it later in this section.

**EXAMPLE 3—**

$f(x) = 3x + 5$      $f(4) = 3(4) + 5 = 15$

This is an example of a *linear function*, or simply a **line!**

**EXAMPLE 4—**

$f(x) = 3^x$      $D = \{4, 0, -2\}$

$f(4) = 3^4 = 81$      $f(0) = 3^0 = 1$      $f(-2) = 3^{-2} = 1/3^2 = 1/9)$      Range $= \{81, 1, 1/9\}$

This is an example of an *exponential function*. We will also talk a little about this later in this section.

## PROBLEMS

**PROBLEM 1—**

If $f(x) = 3x + 7$, and $f(x) = 4$, $x =$

A. 19    B. 7    C. 3    D. 0    E. −1

**PROBLEM 2—**

If $g(x) = x^2 + 7$ and $g(x) = 16$, $x =$

A. 3    B. ±3    C. ±$\sqrt{3}$    D. 4    E. ±4

**PROBLEM 3—**

If $F(x) = 2^x$ and $F(x) = 16$, then $F(x/4) =$

A. 0    B. 1    C. 2    D. 4    E. 16

**PROBLEM 4—**

If $f(x) = x^2 + 3x$, $g(x) = x^2 - 2x + 10$, and $f(x) = g(x)$,
then $x =$

A. 1    B. 2    C. −2    D. 3    E. 1

**Problems 5–8.**   $f(2) = 3$ and $f(5) = 9$.

**PROBLEM 5—**

The distance between these two points in the square
root of what?

**PROBLEM 6—**

The slope between these two points is what?

**PROBLEM 7—**

The value of the y intercept of the line joining these
two points is

A. −1    B. 0    C. 2    D. 5    E. 9

**PROBLEM 8—**

The sum of the coordinates of the midpoint of the line
segment joining these two points is what?

**Problems 9–11.**   $f(x) = 4 - x^2$ and $g(x) = x^2 - 9$.

**PROBLEM 9—**

The difference between the larger x intercept of f(x) and the smaller x intercept of g(x) is what?

**PROBLEM 10—**

The distance between the vertex of f(x) and the vertex of g(x) is what?

**PROBLEM 11—**

$-|3f(x) + 3g(x)| = ?$

**PROBLEM 12—**

$f(x) = x^2 + 6x + 12.$   If $f(x) = 3$, then $x =$

A. $-3$     B. 0     C. 6     D. 12     E. 39

**PROBLEM 13—**

$f(x + 2) = x^2 + 7;$   $f(5) =$

A. 32     B. 16     C. 11     D. 8     E. 7

**PROBLEM 14—**

$f(x) = 2x + 2^x. f(5) - f(3) =$

A. $f(1) + 1$       B. $f(2) + 2$       C. $f(3) + 3$
D. $f(4) + 4$       E. $f(5) + 5$

# SOLUTIONS

**PROBLEM 1—**

$3x + 7 = 4; x = -1.$

The answer is E.

**PROBLEM 2—**

$x^2 + 7 = 16; x^2 = 9; x = 3$ and $-3.$

The answer is B.

**PROBLEM 3—**

$2^x = 16$; $x = 4$; $F(x/4) = 2^{x/4} = 2^{4/4} = 2^1 = 2$.

The answer is C.

**PROBLEM 4—**

$x^2 + 3x = x^2 - 2x + 10$; $3x = -2x + 10$. $5x = 10$; $x = 2$.

The answer is B.

**Problems 5–8.**   Let $f(2) = 3$ and $f(5) = 9$.

**PROBLEM 5—**

$f(2) = 3$ and $f(5) = 9$ means we have the points $(2, 3)$ and $(5, 9)$. We do not need the square root sign. $(5 - 2)^2 + (9 - 3)^2 = 45$.

**PROBLEM 6—**

The slope $m = \dfrac{9 - 3}{5 - 2} = 2$.

**PROBLEM 7—**

Let $m = 2$ and choose $x = 2$ and $y = 3$; $y = mx + b$ is $3 = (2)(2) + b$; $b = -1$.

The answer is A.

**PROBLEM 8—**

The midpoint of $(2, 3)$ and $(5, 9) = \left(\dfrac{2 + 5}{2}, \dfrac{3 + 9}{2}\right) = (3.5, 6)$. $3.5 + 6 = 9.5$ or $19/2$.

**Problems 9–11.**   Let $f(x) = 4 - x^2$ and $g(x) = x^2 - 9$.

**PROBLEM 9—**

The x intercepts of $f(x)$ is $f(x) = 0$; $x = 2$ and $-2$; 2 the larger. For $g(x)$ we have $x = 3$ and $-3$, the smaller is $-3$. $2 - (-3) = 5$.

**PROBLEM 10—**

The distance between $(0, 4)$ and $(0, -9)$ is $4 - (-9) = 13$.

**PROBLEM 11—**

$3f(x) + 3\ g(x) = 3(4 - x^2) + 3(x^2 - 9) = -15$;
$|-15| = 15; - |-15| = -15$.

**PROBLEM 12—**

$x^2 + 6x + 12 = 9; x^2 + 6x + 9 = (x + 3)^2 = 0$;
$x = -3$.
The answer is A.

**PROBLEM 13—**

$x + 2 = 5; x = 3; 3^2 + 7 = B$.

**PROBLEM 14—**

$f(5) = 2(5) + 2^5 = 42; f(3) = 2(3) + 2^3 = 14; 42 - 14 =$
$28; f(4) + 4 = 2(4) + 2^4 + 4 = 28$.

The answer is D.

Let's talk some more.

**EXAMPLE 5—**

Find the domain and range for $f(x) = \sqrt{x - 5}$.

*Answer:* The range is easy. $y = f(x)$ can't be negative.
So $y \geq 0$.

You can't take the square root of a negative number. $x$
$- 5 \geq 0$ or $x \geq 5$, the domain.

**EXAMPLE 6—**

Find the range and domain for $f(x) = \dfrac{1}{\sqrt{x - 5}}$

*Answer:* Since the square root is on the bottom, $y$ can't
be zero. The range is $y > 0$.

Since $y$ can't be zero, $x$ can't be 5. The domain is $x > 5$.

**EXAMPLE 7—**

Find the range and domain for $f(x) = \dfrac{x-5}{x-3}$.

*Answer:* In this case, it is easier to see what x can't be. The bottom of a fraction can't be 0.

The domain is all x except 3, written $x \neq 3$. To find the range, we have to solve for x.

$\dfrac{y}{1} = \dfrac{x-5}{x-3}.\ y(x-3) = x-5.\ xy - 3y = x - 5.\ xy - x$

$= 3y - 5.\ x(y-1) = 3y - 5.\ x = \dfrac{3y-5}{y-1}.$

We see that y can't be one. The range is $y \neq 1$.

**NOTE**

For those who have taken curve sketching with asymptotes, what y can't be is the location of the horizontal asymptote.

## LET'S TRY SOME MORE QUESTIONS

**PROBLEM 15—**

If $f(3) = 4$ and $f(5) = 7$, find the slope of the line through these two points.

**PROBLEM 16—**

If $f(x) = x^2 - 3x + 4$ and $f(x) = 4$, then $x =$

A. 0     B. 3     C. 4     D. 0 and 3     E. 8

**PROBLEM 17—**

The domain of $f(x) = \dfrac{x}{x^2 - 4}$ is all values of x except:

A. 0 and 0     B. 2     C. 2 and −2     D. 2, −2,

E. 2 and 0

## SOLUTIONS

### PROBLEM 15—

f(3) = 4 means the point (3, 4). The other point is
(5, 7). m = $\dfrac{7 - 4}{5 - 3}$ = $\dfrac{3}{2}$.

### PROBLEM 16—

$x^2 - 3x + 4 = 4$. Soo, $x^2 - 3x = 0$. Orrr, x(x − 3) = 0.
x = 0 and 3, D. Trial and error is OK also.

### PROBLEM 17—

The bottom only can't be 0. The answer is C, C, C.

## C. VARIATION

Another new topic that has been added to the SAT is
variation. There are two methods to do the two kinds
of variation. We will do both.

We say y varies directly as x if y = kx, "y equals a constant times x."

If x, y, and k are positive the picture looks like this:

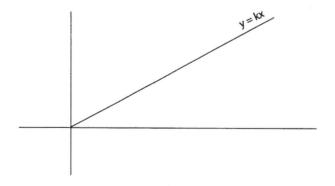

We say y varies inversely as x if y = k/x, "y equals a constant divided by x."

If x, y, and k are positive, the picture looks like this:

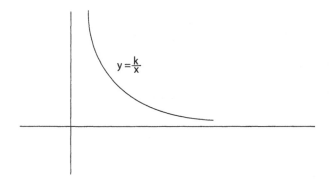

### EXAMPLE 1—

y varies directly as x. If y = 24 when x is 6, find y if x is 5.

*Answer:*

**METHOD 1**
y = kx. 24 = k(6). k = 4. y = 4x. y = 4(5) = 20.

**METHOD 2**
y/x = y/x. 24/6 = y/5. y/5 = 4. y = 20. (You could also cross multiply.)

### EXAMPLE 2—

y varies inversely as x. If y = 6 if x is 4, find y if x is 8.

*Answer:*

**METHOD 1**
y = k/x. 6 = k/4. Sooo, k = 24. y = 24/x. y = 24/8 = 3.

**METHOD 2**

$xy = xy$. $(6)(4) = 8y$. $y = 3$.

You might have more than one variation in a problem. It would be called *joint* variation.

## LET'S TRY SOME PROBLEMS

**EXAMPLE 1—**

y varies inversely as x. If we multiply x by 3, what happens to y?

A.  y is multiplied by 9.        B.  y is multiplied by 3.
C.  y remains the same.        D.  y is divided by 3.
E.  y is divided by 9.

**EXAMPLE 2—**

y varies directly as the square of x. If we multiply x by 10, what happens to y?

A.  y is multiplied by 100.    B.  y is multiplied by 10.
C.  y stays the same.          D.   y is divided by 10.
E.  y is divided by 100.

**EXAMPLE 3—**

y varies directly as the square of x. Its graph looks like what?

A.  line        B.  parabola        C.  circle
D.  square        E.  rectangle

## SOLUTIONS

**EXAMPLE 1—**

The answer is D. Say $y = 30/x$. If $x = 1$, then $y = 30$. Multiply $x = 1$ by 3. Then $y = 30/3 = 10$.

y has been divided by 3, D.

**EXAMPLE 2**

The answer is A. Say $y = 2x^2$. If $x = 1$, then $y = 2$. If $x = 10$, then $y = 200$. It has been multiplied by 100 or 10 squared!

**EXAMPLE 3**

The answer is B, a parabola.

# D. SETS, SETS, SETS

Sets is one of the new topics added to the SAT. We need some basic terms.

A **set** is a collection of "things" called **elements**.

A capital letter, such as S, indicates a set. Small letters indicate elements.

When you write a set, you use braces: { }.

For example, {2, 5, 6} is a set that has three elements: 2, 5, and 6.

$6 \in \{2, 5, 6\}$ means 6 is *an element* in the set.

$7 \notin \{2, 5, 6\}$ means 7 is ***not*** *an element* in the set.

∅ or { } means the *null set* or *empty set*.

For example: The set of all 25-foot human beings is the null set.

Warning! {0}: A set with 1 element in it, the number zero. It is not, not, not the null set!

A∪B, read "A union B," is the set of all elements in A or in B or in both.

A∩B, read "A intersect B" or "A intersection B," is the set of all elements in both sets.

**NOTE:** () are parentheses. [ ] are brackets.

**NOTE** ∈ is the Greek letter epsilon.

**NOTE:** A line through a symbol generally means not. Example: ≠ is not equal.

**NOTE:** ∅ is the Greek, letter phi.

### EXAMPLE 1

Let A = {1, 2, 4, 7}, B = {2, 5, 7, 8}, and C = {3, 5, 6}.

A∪B = {1, 2, 4, 5, 7, 8}. A∩B = {2, 7}. A∩C = ∅. Such sets are called **disjoint**.

### EXAMPLE 2

A = {3, 5}, B = {5, 3}, and C = {3, 3, 5, 3, 5, 5, 3, 5}.

A = B since order does not matter in a set.

A = C since repeated elements count only once. Notice set C has only 2 elements!!!

We say A is a subset of B, written A⊆B, if every element in A is also in B.

### EXAMPLE 3

{4, 7} ⊆ {7, 1, 4, 100}.

If there are n elements in a set, then there are $2^n$ subsets.

### EXAMPLE 4

List all the subsets of {a, b, c}.

*Answer:* The set has 3 elements. There are $2^3$ or 8 subsets.

They are ∅, {a}, {b}, {c}, {a, b}, {a, c}, {b, c}, and {a, b, c}.

## LET'S TRY SOME QUESTIONS

### EXAMPLE 1

A = {1, 2, 3, 4} and B = {3, 4, 5}. A ∪ B =

a. $\{3, 4\}$    b. $\{1, 2, 3, 4, 5\}$    c. $\{4, 5, 6, 7, 8, 9\}$
d. $\varnothing$    e. none of these

**EXAMPLE 2—**

$A = \{5, 6, 7, 8, 9\}$ and $B = \{2, 3, 4, 5, 6\}$. $A \cap B =$

a. $\{5, 6\}$    b. $\{2, 3, 4, 5, 6, 7, 8, 9\}$    c. $\{2, 3, 4, 5, 5, 6, 6, 7, 8, 9\}$    d. $\{10, 18, 28, 40, 54\}$    e. $\varnothing$

**EXAMPLE 3—**

The union of the odd integers and the even integers is

a. all real numbers    b. all counting numbers
c. all integers    d. all rational numbers
e. $\varnothing$

**EXAMPLE 4—**

The intersection of all nonnegative integers and all nonpositive integers is

a. $\varnothing$    b. $\{ \}$    c. $\{0\}$    d. all integers
e. all real numbers

**EXAMPLE 5—**

The intersection of the x axis and the y axis is

a. all points (x, 0) or (0, y)    b. the x-y plane
c. all ordered pairs    d. the origin
e. none of these

**EXAMPLE 6—**

Given $\{a, b, c, d\}$. How many subsets are there not counting the null set and the set itself?

A. 18    B. 17    C. 16    D. 15
E. 14

## SOLUTIONS

**EXAMPLE 1—**

The answer is b. *Union* means put all elements that have appeared once in one set.

**EXAMPLE 2—**

The answer is a. *Intersection* means common to both sets.

**EXAMPLE 3—**

The answer is c.

**EXAMPLE 4—**

The answer is c. *Nonnegative* means 0, 1, 2, 3, 4, . . . *Nonpositive* means 0, −1, −2, −3 . . .

They both have zero in common.

**EXAMPLE 5—**

The answer is d. They meet at the origin (0, 0).

**EXAMPLE 6—**

EEEEE. 4 elements, $2^4$ or 16 subsets. $16 - 2 = 14$.

# E. AVERAGES REVISITED

Some basic statistics have been added to the SAT. We need a few definitions.

**Mean** (*average*):   Add up all the numbers and divide by that number. It is the way your average is determined in school.

**Median** (*average*):   It is the middle number if you are averaging an odd number in the average. It is the average (mean) of the middle two numbers if we have an even number in the average.

**Mode** (*average*):   The most common number; you can have more than one mode.

**Range** (*statistical*):   The largest number minus the smallest number in a set of data.

OK. We are ready.

**EXAMPLE 1—**

Find the mean, median, mode, and range for 4, 4, 4, 8, 9, 11, and 12.

*Answer:* If they are not arranged in order, you must put them in order.

*Range:*   $12 - 4 = 8$. *Mode*: 4, the most common.

*Mean:*   $(4 + 4 + 4 + 8 + 9 + 11 + 12)/7 = 52/7 = 7\ 3/7$.

*Median:*   There are 7 numbers, odd. The median is the middle: 8.

**EXAMPLE 2—**

Find the mean, median, mode, and range for 5, 5, 7, 10, 11, and 11.

*Answer:*   *Range*: $11 - 5 = 6$. *Mode*: There are two: 5 and 11. This is sometimes called *bimodal*.

*Mean:*   $(5 + 5 + 7 + 10 + 11 + 11)/6 = 49/6 = 8\ 1/6$.

*Median:*   There is an even number. The middle two are 7 and 10. $(7 + 10)/2 = 8\ 1/2$.

**EXAMPLE 3—**

{3, 4, 5, 5, 13}. The median minus the mode is

A. −1      B. 0      C. 1      D. 2      E. 5

*Answer:* The middle score is 5. The mode is 5. $5 - 5 = 0$. The answer is B.

## F.   MATRICES

We need to know a few more things for the SAT. The first is matrices.

**Matrix** (plural **matrices**):   In our case it is an array of numbers or letters.

$\begin{bmatrix} 1 & 2 & 4 \\ 0 & -1 & 3 \end{bmatrix}$ is a 2 by 3 matrix, written 2 × 3.

The 2 rows: Row 1 is [1   2   4]. Row 2 is [0   −1   3].

The 3 columns: Column 1 is $\begin{bmatrix} 1 \\ 0 \end{bmatrix}$. Column 2 is $\begin{bmatrix} 2 \\ -1 \end{bmatrix}$. Column 3 is $\begin{bmatrix} 4 \\ 3 \end{bmatrix}$.

There are three operations you need to know:

1.   A number on the outside multiplies each entry in the matrix.

$$4\begin{bmatrix} 3 & -1 \\ 0 & a \end{bmatrix} = \begin{bmatrix} 12 & -4 \\ 0 & 4a \end{bmatrix}$$

2.   When matrices are added, their rows and columns must be the same. When adding, you add the corresponding entry.

**EXAMPLE 1—**

$$\begin{bmatrix} a & b \\ c & d \\ e & f \end{bmatrix} + \begin{bmatrix} g & h \\ i & j \\ k & l \end{bmatrix} = \begin{bmatrix} a+g & b+h \\ c+i & d+j \\ e+k & f+l \end{bmatrix}$$

**EXAMPLE 2—**

$$\begin{bmatrix} 1 & 2 & 3 \\ 4 & 5 & 6 \\ 7 & 8 & -9 \end{bmatrix} + \begin{bmatrix} 1 & -2 & 5 \\ 0 & -5 & 4 \\ 6 & 2 & 8 \end{bmatrix} = \begin{bmatrix} 2 & 0 & 8 \\ 4 & 0 & 10 \\ 13 & 10 & -1 \end{bmatrix}$$

3.   Multiplying is trickier. In order to multiply matrices, the number of columns in the first must be the same as the number of rows in the second.
If you multiply an m × n matrix with an n × p matrix, the result is an n × p matrix.

**EXAMPLE 3—**

Suppose A is a 2 × 3 matrix, and B is a 3 × 2 matrix, AB would be 2 × 2, aaand BA would be a 3 × 3 matrix. Let's do it!!!!!!

$$A = \begin{bmatrix} a & b & c \\ d & e & f \end{bmatrix} \text{ and } B = \begin{bmatrix} g & j \\ h & k \\ i & l \end{bmatrix}$$

$$AB = \begin{bmatrix} ag+bh+ci & aj+bk+cl \\ dg+eh+fi & dj+ek+fl \end{bmatrix}$$

$$B = \begin{bmatrix} g & j \\ h & k \\ i & l \end{bmatrix} \text{ and } A = \begin{bmatrix} a & b & c \\ d & e & f \end{bmatrix}$$

$$BA = \begin{bmatrix} ga + jd & gb + je & gc + jf \\ ha + kd & hb + ke & hc + kf \\ ia + ld & ib + le & ic + lf \end{bmatrix}$$

Notice this is the first kind of multiplication that is **not** commutative. The order of multiplication **does** make a difference!

## G. TRANSLATING TRANSLATIONS

No, this is not changing Spanish into French. This part involves horizontal and vertical movements without changing the shape of the object.

Here we will be discussing translation of a basic parabola, specifically $y = x^2$.

The picture of this curve looks like this:

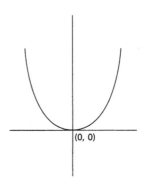

The rounded point is called the *vertex*. In this case the vertex is at the point (0, 0).

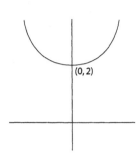

The curve y = x² + 2 is a shift 2 units up.

Its vertex is at the point (0, 2). Its picture is this:

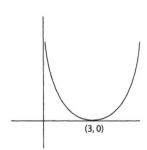

The curve y = (x − 3)² is a shift 3 units to the right.

Its vertex is (3, 0). Its picture looks like this:

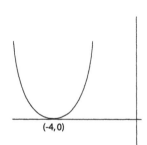

The curve y = (x + 4)² is a shift 4 units to the left.

Its vertex is (−4, 0). Its picture looks like this:

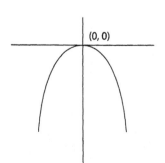

The curve y = −x² looks like this:

It is the same as y = x² except **upside down!**

In drawing $y = x^2$, $y = (1/2)x^2$, and $y = 2x^2$ on the same graph, the coefficient in front determines how fast the parabola goes up. They are pictured here:

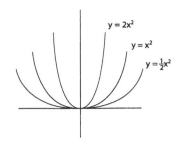

**EXAMPLE 1**

When $y = (x - 1)^2$ and $y = (x - 7)^2$ meet, the y coordinate of that point is

A. 1　　　B. 3　　　C. 4　　　D. 7　　　E. 9

**EXAMPLE 2**

The distance between the vertices of $y = x^2 - 4$ and $y = 4 - x^2$ is

A. 0　　　B. 4　　　C. 8　　　D. 16　　　E. 256

## SOLUTIONS

**EXAMPLE 1**

You can solve this algebraically, but it takes way too much time!

If you look at the pictures, they are equidistant from the middle of $x = 1$ and $x = 7$:

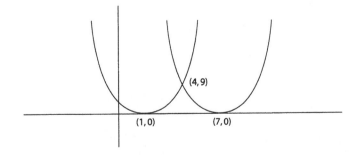

So $x = 4$. If $x = 4$, then $y = 9$, E.

EXAMPLE 2—

The vertex of this first parabola is (0, −4); the second is (0, 4).

The distance between them is 8, C.

To learn more on parabolas, visit *Precalc with Trig for the Clueless.* For more on translations, see *Geometry for the Clueless.*

# H. RIGHT ANGLE TRIGONOMETRY

For the SAT you need to know a teeny-weeny amount of trig.

The right triangle to the right has right angle C and hypotenuse $\overline{AB}$.

Sine A, abbreviated sin A $= \dfrac{\text{opposite side}}{\text{hypotenuse}} = \dfrac{\overline{BC}}{\overline{AB}}$.

Cosine A, abbreviated cos A $= \dfrac{\text{adjacent side}}{\text{hypotenuse}} = \dfrac{\overline{AC}}{\overline{AB}}$.

Tangent A, abbreviated tan A $= \dfrac{\text{opposite side}}{\text{adjacent side}} = \dfrac{\overline{BC}}{\overline{AC}}$.

EXAMPLE—

Given the triangle below:

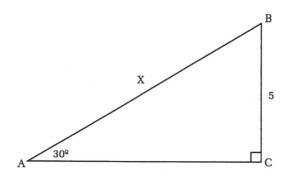

The hypotenuse is what?

*Answer:* sin 30° = 5/hypotenuse. 1/2 = 5/x; x = 10.

You can use the fact that in a 30°, 60°, 90° triangle, the hypotenuse is twice the short leg, a fact you learned earlier in this book or in *Geometry for the Clueless*.

**NOTE I**

If you want to learn more about trig, see *Precalc with Trig for the Clueless*.

**NOTE 2**

A memory device for the trig functions is the Indian chief SOHCAHTOA: Sine is Opposite over Hypotenuse, Cosine is Adjacent over Hypotenuse, and Tangent is Opposite over Adjacent. It was the only thing my father remembered from trig, which he learned 2864 years ago. Almost everything that stands the test of time has value.

**NOTE 3**

With the exception of one topic, trig should be the easiest course you ever take when done properly.

**NOTE 4**

Since trig on the SAT is only used in relation to the 30°, 60°, 90° triangle and the 45°, 45°, 90° triangle, I would not even use trig on the SAT. I would use the facts I learned about these two triangles. You decide for yourself.

# I. EXPONENTIAL GROWTH AND DECAY

Exponential growth and decay is really part of a topic called *geometric progressions*. The way you tell if a sequence of numbers is a geometric progression is that there is one number that multiplies a term to get the next term.

### EXAMPLE 1

6, 12, 24, 48, . . . , is a geometric progression.

The first term, sometimes denoted by the letter a, is 6; a = 6.

The common number multiplied, denoted by the letter r (for ratio), is 2.

This example is an *exponential growth* since the terms increase and r > 1.

### EXAMPLE 2

81, 27, 9, 3, . . . , is a geometric progression; a = 81 and r = 1/3.

This is an *exponential decay* since the numbers decrease and 0 < r < 1.

### EXAMPLE 3

$8 \times 3^n$ is an exponential growth formula.

The first term is a = 8, and r = 3. Written out, the sequence is 8, 24, 72, 216 . . .

### EXAMPLE 4

We have a population growth of $1000 \times 6^{t/10}$; t is in years.

There are 1000 people originally; every 10 years, the population is multiplied by 6. Why?

If t = 10, substituting, we get $1000 \times 6^{10/10} = 1000 \times 6^1 = 1000 \times 6 = 6000$!

**EXAMPLE 5—**

We have a radioactive decay of $64 \times \left(\frac{1}{2}\right)^{t/5}$; t is in minutes.

We start with 64 pounds of a substance; in 5 minutes 1/2 of it, 32 pounds, is still radioactive.

Here is a question the SAT might ask.

**EXAMPLE 6—**

We have 800 pounds of a radioactive substance. Its half-life is 10 minutes.

How much radioactive stuff (the SAT never says "stuff") is left in an hour?

*Answer:* 800 radioactive pounds at the start, 400 left after 10 minutes (that's what half-life is—losing 1/2); 200 after 20 minutes, 100 after 30 minutes, 50 after 40 minutes, 25 after 50 minutes, and 12.5 pounds of radioactive stuff left after an hour, the answer.

Oh, let's try one more.

**EXAMPLE 7—**

Tinyville USA has a population of 400. Its population is multiplied by 4 every 20 years.

When will Tinyville have a population of 3200?

*Answer:* The population, given by $400 \times 4^{t/20}$, must equal 3200. Divide both sides by 400.

We get $4^{t/20} = 8$. $4 = 2^2$ and $8 = 2^3$. Soooo, $(2^2)^{t/20} = 2^{t/10} = 2^3$. $t/10 = 3$; $t = 30$ years!

Let's practice our skills with three SAT-like tests. But first, here are a few things you might like to know about the SAT.

## CHAPTER 20

# PRACTICING FOR THE MATH SAT

Congratulations on finishing the book. You are now ready to do the practice SATs. They are designed with questions that are similar to the kinds of questions on the real SATs. But there are some differences you should know.

1. The regular SATs are dull and boring. Mine are written so that you can have some fun with them. Hopefully, the day of the SAT you will remember these tests and laugh a little. Relaxing makes scores better.

2. If you notice, I don't put the formulas on the top of each section like the SAT. If you need to look, you will not do well. You must have the formulas memorized, you must.

3. You'll notice that the answer sheets I've provided don't look like the SAT answer sheets. Use mine for taking practice tests in this book because they are easy to use; but make sure you now how to use the SAT answer sheet before you take the actual SAT test.

4. Do not take the time limits on my tests too seriously. ETS, the maker of the SATs, has a very large staff and pretests all the questions. I am a staff of one.

5. The SATs have more reading-type questions (usually) than I do. Since they are one of a kind, I have not done as many because they probably won't do you much good. However, the SAT does give once-in-a-lifetime surprise kinds of questions. I did put in a few of these.

6. Also, my tests may be a little harder than the real SATs since I have not put in as many easy questions as the SAT. Annnd, since the SAT pretests all of the problems, it can put them in order, easy to hard. I have tried, but I don't guarantee the order of difficulty.

Incidentally, I have great respect for ETS. The hardest thing I have evvvver written is a math SAT. It is so hard you wouldn't believe!!!!

Just like before, after each test or each part of each test, read the solutions and make sure you understand each problem. Good luck!!!!!

## CHAPTER 21

# PRACTICE TEST I

## PART I

Use the empty spaces on these pages to do all of your
scratch work. When you decide which choice is correct, fill in its letter A, B, C, D, or E on the answer
sheet at the end of this chapter. On the real SAT, you
will fill in a circle.

25 questions, 30 minutes

1. $9 - x = x - 9$. $x =$
   A. $-9$
   B. $0$
   C. $9$
   D. $18$
   E. $81$

2. $x =$
   A. $30°$
   B. $40°$
   C. $70°$
   D. $110°$
   E. $290°$

   $L_1 \parallel L_2$

   $30°$
   $x$
   $40°$
   $L_1$
   $L_2$

   Go on to the next page
   now!!!! Do not hesitate.

**199**

3. $(3x^2)^2(2x^3)^3 =$

    A. $6x^{13}$

    B. $6x^{10}$

    C. $72x^{10}$

    D. $72x^{13}$

    E. $5x^{36}$

4. If Sandy paid $14 for 4 tickets, how much do 6 tickets cost?

    A. $7

    B. $14

    C. $21

    D. $28

    E. $56

5. y is 7 less than 3 times x. Then $x =$

    A. $(y + 7)/3$

    B. $(y - 7)/3$

    C. $3y + 7$

    D. $3y - 7$

    E. $7/3 - y/3$

6. If $x + 9$ is an even integer, the sum of the next two even integers is

    A. $x + 11$

    B. $2x + 22$

    C. $2x + 24$

    D. $3x + 39$

    E. $x^2 + 24x + 143$

7. If $\dfrac{3x}{4} = 5$, then $\dfrac{3x}{5} =$

   A. 20
   B. 20/3
   C. 3
   D. 4
   E. 5

8. If a £ b = ab − b + b², then 3 £ 5 =

   A. 2
   B. 8
   C. 15
   D. 21
   E. 35

9. A board of length 45 feet is sawed into 2 pieces that are in the ratio of 2:3. The length of the larger piece is

   A. 9
   B. 18
   C. 27
   D. 36
   E. 45

10. 200000000000000000000000000000006 is exactly divisible by

   A. 2
   B. 3
   C. 9
   D. 2 and 3
   E. 2, 3, and 9

Go on to the next page.

11. $\sqrt{100 - 64} =$

   A. 2
   B. 3
   C. 4
   D. 6
   E. 8

12. If $x = -3$, then $-x^2 =$

   A. 6
   B. -6
   C. 9
   D. -9
   E. 81

13. x years in the future, Sandy will be y years old. z years in the future, Sandy will be how old?

   A. $x + y + z$
   B. $x - y + z$
   C. $x - y - z$
   D. $x + z$
   E. $y - x + z$

14. $\overline{AB}$ is parallel to $\overline{CD}$, annnd $\overline{AD}$ is parallel to $\overline{BC}$. Angle A = 2x degrees. Angle C = 4x − 80 degrees. Angle B is how many degrees?

   A. 40°
   B. 80°
   C. 100°
   D. 110°
   E. 120°

15. $\dfrac{x}{y} = -2$    $x + y =$

 A. $-2y$
 B. $0$
 C. $-y$
 D. $3y$
 E. $-3y$

16. 20 students received a 90 on a math test. 30 students got 100 on the same test. The class average (arithmetic mean) is

 A. 92
 B. 94
 C. 95
 D. 96
 E. 98

17. Let a, b, c, d, e, f, g, and h be positive integers from 1 through 9, but we are not telling you what they are. a b c d 9 is exactly divisible by e f 7. The quotient could be

 A. g h 3
 B. g h 4
 C. g h 5
 D. g h 6
 E. g h 7

18. $10^{100} = 100^x$. $x =$

 A. 50
 B. 100
 C. 110
 D. 1000
 E. 10

Go, go, go to the next page. Now!!!!

19. Given point P is on a line. A and B, not pictured, are on opposite sides of P such that $3\overline{AP} = 4\overline{PB}$. M is the midpoint of $\overline{AP}$.

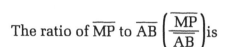

The ratio of $\overline{MP}$ to $\overline{AB}$ $\left(\dfrac{\overline{MP}}{\overline{AB}}\right)$ is

A. 3/4
B. 4/3
C. 2/7
D. 2/5
E. 5/2

20. The sum of 5 consecutive integers is 105. The sum of the first 2 is

A. 19
B. 21
C. 39
D. 41
E. 43

21. A jar contains 4 letter A's, 2 letter B's, and 5 letter E's. If a letter is pulled out at random, the probability of picking a vowel is

A. 9/11
B. 2/11
C. 2/3
D. 11/4
E. 3/2

22. $\dfrac{\dfrac{4}{7} + \dfrac{1}{2}}{\dfrac{4}{7} - \dfrac{1}{2}} =$

A. 15
B. 1

C. 0

D. 5/3

E. 3/5

23. $x = 2^{7n}$. $16x =$

  A. $32^{7n}$

  B. $2^{112n}$

  C. $2^{7n+4}$

  D. $2^{28n}$

  E. $2^{11n}$

24. $-1 < x < 0$. Arrange $x^3$, $x^4$, $x^5$ in order, smallest to largest.

  A. $x^3 < x^4 < x^5$

  B. $x^3 < x^5 < x^4$

  C. $x^5 < x^4 < x^3$

  D. $x^5 < x^3 < x^4$

  E. $x^4 < x^3 < x^5$

25. The center of the circle is O.

  $$\overline{CD} = \overline{EF} = \overline{GH} = \frac{1}{2}\overline{FH} = \frac{1}{2}\overline{BG} = 12$$

  The area of the shaded portion is

  A. $72\sqrt{3} - 36\pi$

  B. $72\sqrt{3} - 18\pi$

  C. $72\sqrt{3} - 12\pi$

  D. $36\sqrt{3} - 18\pi$

  E. $36\sqrt{3} - 12\pi$

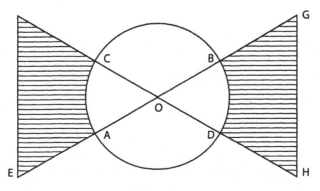

Stop, Stop! Stop!!!! Do NOT go on!!!!

## PART 2

Use any empty space on these test pages to do your scratch work. Then decide which of the five answers is correct. Fill in letter A, B, C, D, or E on the answer sheet at the end of this chapter. On the real SAT, you will fill in a circle.

25 questions, 30 minutes

1. 240 radioactive grams of goo loses half its radioactivity every 10 days. How many grams of radioactive goo is left in 40 days?

   A. 120
   B. 60
   C. 30
   D. 15
   E. none

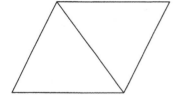

2. A rhombus is made from 2 equilateral triangles. One side is $\sqrt[4]{3}$. The area is

   A. 1/4
   B. 1/2
   C. 1
   D. 3/2
   E. 2

*For Problems 3 and 4:* $f(x) = 5(x - 3)^2$ And $g(x) = 5(x + 1)^2.$

3. The x value that makes $f(x) = g(x)$ is

   A. x = 20
   B. x = 3
   C. x = 1
   D. x = 0
   E. x = −1

4. The y value that makes $f(x) = g(x)$ is

A. $y = 20$
B. $y = 10$
C. $y = 3$
D. $y = 1$
E. $y = -1$

5. If we multiply the matrix $\begin{bmatrix} a & b & c \\ d & e & f \end{bmatrix}$ by $\begin{bmatrix} g \\ h \\ i \end{bmatrix}$, the answer would look like

A. $\begin{bmatrix} p & q & r \\ s & t & u \end{bmatrix}$

B. $\begin{bmatrix} x \\ y \\ z \end{bmatrix}$

C. $\begin{bmatrix} v \\ w \end{bmatrix}$

D. $[j \ k]$

E. can't be done

6. $A-B$ is defined as all elements in A but not in B.
$A = \{1, 2, 3, 4\}$, and $B = \{3, 4, 5\}$. $A-B \cup B-A =$

A. $\{1, 2, 3, 4, 5\}$
B. $\{3, 4\}$
C. $\{1, 2, 5\}$
D. $\{1, 4\}$
E. $\{2, 5\}$

7. $|2x - 2| = x$. $x =$

A. only 2
B. only 2/3
C. only 2 or 2/3
D. only 2, 2/3, or 0
E. all values

8. $x^{-3} = 1/64$; $x^{1/2} =$

A. 2
B. 1
C. 1/2

Go on to the next page.

D. 1/4

E. −2

9. If you multiply the height in a cylinder by 9, by what must you multiply the radius if the volume is to stay the same?

A. 81

B. 9

C. 3

D. 1/3

E. 1/81

10. Given a 30°, 60°, 90° triangle. The largest side is 10. The side opposite the 60° angle is

A. 5

B. $5\sqrt{2} \approx 7.0$

C. $5\sqrt{3} \approx 8.5$

D. $10\sqrt{2} \approx 14$

E. $10\sqrt{3} \approx 17$

11. $\sqrt{x + 6} = x.$  $x =$

A. ±3

B. 3

C. 3, −2

D. −2

E. no integer answer

12. The domain of $f(x) = \dfrac{x}{x^2 - 4}$ is all real numbers except for $x =$

A. 2

B. 2 and −2

C. 0

D. 0, 2, and −2

E. It is true for all values of x.

13. Given the sequence 0, 1, 2, 3, 4, 0, 1, 2, . . . . The 87th term in the sequence is

A. 0

B. 1

C. 2
D. 3
E. 4

14. The number of prime numbers between 70 and 80 is

A. 0
B. 1
C. 2
D. 3
E. 4

15. A car travels 40 mi/h in one direction and returns at 60 mi/h. The average speed is

A. 45 mi/h
B. 48 mi/h
C. 50 mi/h
D. 52 mi/h
E. 55 mi/h

16. If $a^5 > a^3$ and $a > 0$, find a value for a that will make this inequality true.

17. The area of a circle is $36\pi$. If half the circumference is $k\pi$, what is the value of k?

18. If $4 \leq n \leq 6$ and $8 \leq m \leq 10$,

find the maximum value of $\dfrac{m+n}{m-n}$.

19. $5b^2 = 25$. Find the value of $5b^6$.

20. The sum of the first 4 primes is what?

21. Find a fraction between 3/43 and 4/43. You may not have a decimal point in the answer. The denominator must be less than 100.

Go on to the next page. Immediately. At once. Don't delay. Right now!!!!

22. The distance between A and B is what?

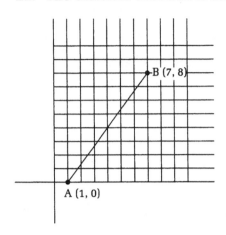

23. Given that there are 12 inches in a foot, the amount of cubic feet of dirt in a rectangular hole that is 6 feet by 6 feet by 9 inches is what?

24. Given the volume of a cone is $(1/3)\pi r^2 h$. The volume of the cylinder pictured is 60. Find the volume of the cone pictured.

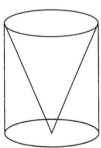

25. A monkey is trying to climb out of a 30-foot hole. In the morning, the monkey climbs up 3 feet. At night, the monkey is so tired he falls back 2 feet. The next day the same thing happens. The morning of what day does the monkey climb out of the hole?

Stop. Halt. Desist. Do NOT go on.

# PART 3

Use any empty space to do your scratch work. Then
decide which of the five answers is correct. Fill in the
letter of the correct answer on the appropriate line
of the answer sheet that is found at the end of this
chapter.

10 questions, 15 minutes

1. $x + 6 = 10$. Then $(x + 3)^2 =$

   A. 4
   B. 16
   C. 20
   D. 49
   E. 64

2. John can duplicate 2000 copies every 90 minutes.
   Mary can make 3000 copies every 90 minutes.
   How many copies can they make in 540 minutes
   if they alternate machines?

   A. 5000
   B. 10,000
   C. 15,000
   D. 20,000
   E. 30,000

3. Which number is the largest?

   A. .10101
   B. .101
   C. .1
   D. .1001
   E. .10011

Go on to the next page.

4. Which of the points below is on a line segment connecting (5, 6) and (21, 18)?

   A. (9, 9)
   B. (12, 12)
   C. (13, 12)
   D. (12, 13)
   E. (16, 15)

5. How many times does the digit 5 appear on integers between 2 and 62?

   A. 5
   B. 6
   C. 15
   D. 16
   E. 17

6. If a mgms costs c cents, then d mgmss costs how many cents?

   A. ad/c
   B. a/dc
   C. dc/a
   D. c/ad
   E. acd

7. Given the list of integers 2, 3, 3, 3, 3, 5, 30, the median minus the mode is

   A. 0
   B. 1
   C. 2
   D. 3
   E. 28

8. $5x + 2y = 10$    $x + 8y = 46$    $3x + 5y =$

    A. 14
    B. 28
    C. 56
    D. 112
    E. impossible to tell

9. $(x + 3)^2 = 6x + 25$

    I. $x = 0$

    II. $x = 4$

    III. $x = -4$    $x =$

    A. I only
    B. II only
    C. III only
    D. I and II
    E. II and III

10. The cube pictured has length of the edge 5. How many distinct paths along the edges from A to B have a length of exactly 15?

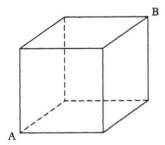

    A. 3
    B. 5
    C. 4
    D. 6
    E. 8

Stop!!!! Let's go to the answers.

# ANSWER SHEET

| Part 1 | Part 2 | Part 3 |
|--------|--------|--------|
| 1. _____ | 1. _____ | 1. _____ |
| 2. _____ | 2. _____ | 2. _____ |
| 3. _____ | 3. _____ | 3. _____ |
| 4. _____ | 4. _____ | 4. _____ |
| 5. _____ | 5. _____ | 5. _____ |
| 6. _____ | 6. _____ | 6. _____ |
| 7. _____ | 7. _____ | 7. _____ |
| 8. _____ | 8. _____ | 8. _____ |
| 9. _____ | 9. _____ | 9. _____ |
| 10. _____ | 10. _____ | 10. _____ |
| 11. _____ | 11. _____ | |
| 12. _____ | 12. _____ | |
| 13. _____ | 13. _____ | |
| 14. _____ | 14. _____ | |
| 15. _____ | 15. _____ | |
| 16. _____ | 16. _____ | |
| 17. _____ | 17. _____ | |
| 18. _____ | 18. _____ | |
| 19. _____ | 19. _____ | |
| 20. _____ | 20. _____ | |
| 21. _____ | 21. _____ | |
| 22. _____ | 22. _____ | |
| 23. _____ | 23. _____ | |
| 24. _____ | 24. _____ | |
| 25. _____ | 25. _____ | |

## CHAPTER 22

# PRACTICE TEST I ANSWERS

## PART I

1. Trial and error will show you the answer is 9
   orrrr $-2x = -18$. So $x = 9$.                          C

2. The secret is to draw the parallel line in the middle:

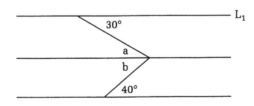

   $a = 30°$

   $b = 40°$

   $x = a + b = 70°$                                        C

3. One way to do it is $(3x^2)(3x^2)(2x^3)(2x^3)(2x^3) = 72x^{13}$.

                                                            D

4. $14 = 4 tickets

$ 7 = 2 tickets

$21 = 6 tickets                                        C

5. Reading it we get y = 3x − 7. Remember, it is the equal sign annnnd less than reverses. Solving for x,

3x − 7 = y

3x       = y + 7

x       = (y + 7)/3                                   A

6. The space between even integers is allllways 2. x + 11 is the next; x + 13 is the next. The sum is 2x + 24.                            C

7. You could solve for x, buuut

$$\frac{3x}{4} = \frac{5}{1}$$

Interchange the 4 and 5, which you can do in a proportion:

$$\frac{3x}{5} = \cdots \frac{4}{1}$$                   D

8. a £ b = ab − b + b². A "follow-the-rules" problem. a = 3; b = 5. a £ b = 3(5) − 5 + 5² = 35.    E

9. The easiest way to do it is 2x + 3x = 45. 5x = 45. x = 9. The larger piece is 3x = 3(9) = 27.    C

10. There are two tricks (actually three) involved. The number is divisible by 2 because the last digit, 6, is even. The sum of allll the digits is 8, which is not divisible by 3 or 9. Soooo, the answer is                                       A

11. Order of operations. $\sqrt{36} = 6$.        D

12. This is a problem I always give because so
    many people get it wrong, even advanced ones.
    $-x^2 = -(-3)(-3) = -9$ (3 minus signs is minus).    D

13. The trick is to put the age NOWWWW. y in x
    years in the future? $y - x$ now. $y - x + z$,
    z years in the future.        E

14. $A = C$. $2x = 4x - 80$. $x = 40°$. Sooo, $A = 80°$.
    B is sup $= 100°$.        C

15. $\dfrac{x}{y} = \dfrac{-2}{1}$     $x = -2y$     $x + y = -2y + y = -y$    C

16. $20(90) = 1800$ points; $30(100) = 3000$ points.
    Total, 4800 points divided by $50 = 96$.     D

17. Why does $486/27 = 18$? Because $27 \times 18 = 486$.
    More specifically, the last digits must multiply.
    The answer is E, since (g h 7)(e f 7) must end in
    a 9 since $7 \times 7 = 49$. The others won't.     E

18. $10^{100} = (10^2)^x$. $2x = 100$. Sooo, $x = 50$.     A

19. $3\,\overline{AP} = 4\,\overline{PB}$. Let $\overline{PB} = 3$ units and $\overline{AP} = 4$ units
    and M is located as pictured. $\overline{MP}/\overline{AB} = 2/7$,
    just count.        C

20. If it is an odd number, the middle is $105/5 =$
    21. First 2 are before 19 and 20. The sum is 39.   C

21. 9 vowels, 2 consonants. 9/11.        A

22. The LCD is 14:

$$\frac{\dfrac{14}{1}\dfrac{4}{7}+\dfrac{14}{1}\dfrac{1}{2}}{\dfrac{14}{1}\dfrac{4}{7}-\dfrac{14}{1}\dfrac{1}{2}}=\frac{8+7}{8-7}=\frac{15}{1}=15 \qquad\qquad A$$

23. $16 = 2^4$. $16x = 2^4 2^{7n} = 2^{7n+4}$, adding the exponents. $\qquad\qquad$ C

24. $x^4$ must be biggest because it is the only positive. Let $x = -1/2$:

$$(-1/2)^3 = -1/8 \qquad (-1/2)^5 = -1/32$$

which is bigger than $-1/8$.

Remember, negatives reverse. Still don't believe? Look! $\qquad\qquad$ B

25. The shaded portion is 2 equilateral triangles minus $\dfrac{1}{3}$ of a circle:

$$2\left(\frac{5^2\sqrt{3}}{4}\right) - \frac{1}{3}\pi r^2.\ S = d = 12;\ r = 6.$$

$$2\left(\frac{12^2\sqrt{3}}{4}\right) - \frac{1}{3}\pi(6)^2 = 72\sqrt{3} - 12\pi. \qquad\qquad C$$

# PART 2

1. In this problem 1/2 life means half the grams are lost every 10 days. In 10 days there will be 120 grams left. In 20 days there will be 60 grams left. In 30 days there will be 30 grams left. In 40 days there will be 15 grams left. $\qquad$ D

2. The area of an equilateral triangle is $s^2\sqrt{3}/4$.

There are two of them; s = $\sqrt[4]{3}$. s² = $(\sqrt[4]{3})^2$ = $\sqrt{3}$.
Sooo 2(s² $\sqrt{3}$/4) = 2($\sqrt{3}$)($\sqrt{3}$)/4 = 3/2.              D

3.   The 5s cancel. We have $(x + 1)^2 = (x - 3)^2$. By
     sight x = 1 since $(2)^2 = (-2)^2$.                  C

4.   $f(1) = 5(1 - 3)^2 = 20$. We could also find g(1).
     They are the same.                                  A

5.   If you multiply a 2-by-3 matrix by a 3-by-1
     matrix, you get a 2 by 1.                           C

6.   A−B = {1, 2}; B−A = {5}. The union of these two
     sets is C.                                          C

7.   You could solve 2x − 2 = x and 2x − 2 = −x or
     substitution.                                       C

8.   $x^{-3} = 4^{-3}$; x = 4; $x^{1/2} = 4^{1/2} = \sqrt{4} = 2$.              A

9.   $V = \pi r^2 h$. The easiest way to do this problem is to
     let r = 1 and h = 1 in the beginning, ignoring pi.
     Sooo, the original r²h = 1. If h = now 9, 9 times 1,
     then for the volume to remain the same r² = 1/9, r
     would have to multiplied by 1/3.                    D

10.  Opposite the 30° angle is 1/2(10) = 5. Opposite
     60° = 5$\sqrt{3}$.                                     C

11.  The easiest way is by substitution.                 B

12.  All numbers are OK except when the bottom is
     not 0: $x^2 - 4 = (x - 2)(x + 2) \neq 0$. So x can't be 2
     or −2.                                              B

13.  The sequence repeats every 5. 87 divided by 5
     has a remainder of 2. The second number in the
     sequence is 1; so the answer is B.                  B

14.  71, 73, and 79 are the primes between 70
     and 80.                                             D

15.  This is a tough question. The average speed is not
     the average of the speeds. 50 is NOT the answer.

The distance is not given. It does not matter. We take 120 miles since 60 and 40 are factors of 120. Time = distance/rate. t = 120/60 = 2 hours; t = 120/40 = 3 hours; speed = total distance / total time = 240/5 = 48 mi/h.                                  B

16. An easy one; any number bigger than 1 is ok.

17. $\pi r^2 = 36\pi$. So r = 6. c = $2\pi r$ = $12\pi$. Half of this is $6\pi$. k = 6.

18. A real toughie. Doesn't fit the patterns we have learned. The max and min values occur at the extremes. So n = 4 or 6, and m = 8 or 10:

$$\frac{10 + 4}{10 - 4} = 14/6 \qquad \frac{10 + 6}{10 - 6} = 16/4 = 4$$

$$\frac{8 + 4}{8 - 4} = 4 \qquad \frac{8 + 6}{8 - 6} = 14/2 = 7.$$

The answer is 7.

19. $5b^6 = 5b^2(b^2)(b^2)$. $5b^2 = 25$. Sooooo, $b^2 = 5$. 25(5)(5) = 625.

20. 2 + 3 + 5 + 7 = 17. 1 is not a prime. 2 is the only even prime.

21. $\frac{3}{43} = \frac{6}{86}$ ; $\frac{4}{43} = \frac{8}{86}$. Between is 7/86.

22. Straight distance formula $\sqrt{(7 - 1)^2 + (8 - 0)^2} = 10$.

23. 0. There is no dirt in a hole. Some of the SAT is just fun.

24. This is much easier than it looks if you see the trick. You don't need to know r or h. Good thing. You can't find them. All you need to know is the volume of a cone is 1/3 the cylinder since h and r are the same. 1/3 of 60 is 20.

25. After 27 days, the monkey has netted 27 feet. On the 28th morning, the monkey climbs 3 feet. 27 + 3 = 30. The monkey is out of the hole on day 28.

# PART 3

1. $x = 4$. $x + 3 = 7$. $7^2 = 49$.          D

2. The trick is "alternate". You must read this word.

2000 + 3000 + 2000 + 3000 + 2000 + 3000 = 15,000.    C

3. These were the choices:

   A. .10101
   B. .10100
   C. .10000
   D. .10010
   E. .10011

The first 2 digits are the same for all. The third digit eliminates C, D, and E. The fifth digit eliminates B.    A

4. $m = (18 - 6)/(21 - 5) = 12/15 = 3/4$. The only point that has same slope with (5, 6) is      A

5. 5, 15, 25, 35, 45, 50, 51, 52, 53, 54, 55 (2 5s), 56, 57, 58, 59          D

6.  $\dfrac{a}{c} = \dfrac{d}{x}.$    $x = dc/a$                    C

7.  The median is the middle, 3. The mode is the most common, 3. $3 - 3 = 0$.                A

8.  Add: $6x + 10y = 56$. Divide by 2. $3x + 5y = 28$.    B

9.  Trial and error, orrr $x^2 + 6x + 9 = 6x + 25$. $x^2 = 16$. $x = \pm 4$.                E

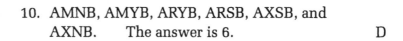

10.  AMNB, AMYB, ARYB, ARSB, AXSB, and AXNB.    The answer is 6.                D

Let's try another test. You have no idea how hard it is to make one of these up. Don't tell me it's harder to take it. I think these are fun to take. Hopefully, after you read this book, you will not only do this book muuuuch better but enjoy doing these problems. Let's go on.

## CHAPTER 23

# PRACTICE TEST II

## PART I

Select the best answer, A, B, C, D, or E, and put it on your form. On the real SAT, you will fill in a circle or something like a circle.

25 questions, 30 minutes

1. $9 - 5x = 5$. $3 - 5x =$

   A. −1
   B. 0
   C. 5
   D. 6
   E. 9

2. $x =$

   A. 30
   B. 50
   C. 55
   D. 65
   E. 110

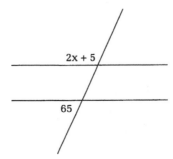

Go immmmediately to the next page!!!!

3. $\dfrac{x}{6} + \dfrac{x}{12} = 2$. $x =$

   A. 2
   B. 4
   C. 6
   D. 8
   E. 12

4. $x - y = 5$. $xy = 24$. $x + y$ could be

   A. 9
   B. 11
   C. 14
   D. 17
   E. 20

5. 1, 3, 6, 10, 15, . . . .What is the 10th term of the sequence?

   A. 40
   B. 50
   C. 55
   D. 61
   E. 72

6. 2 bats and 2 balls costs $48.00. 7 bats and 6 balls costs $182.00. 1 ball and 1 bat costs . . .

   A. $18
   B. $22
   C. $24
   D. $28
   E. $32

7. $\dfrac{x\,(x^{a+b})}{x^b} =$

    A. $(x^2)^{a+2b}$
    B. $x^{2a}$
    C. $x^{a+2b+1}$
    D. $x^{a+1}$
    E. $x^{ab+b^2}$

8. $7x + 5y = 39$. $5x + 3y = 11$. What is $(x + y)/2$?

    A. 7
    B. 14
    C. 18
    D. 21
    E. 28

9. $2^{60} = 8^{4x}$. $x =$

    A. 15
    B. 7.5
    C. 5
    D. 2⅓
    E. 20

10. $(-1)^2 + (-1)^3 + (-1)^4 + (-1)^5 + (-1)^6 + (-1)^7 + (-1)^8 + (-1)^9 + (-1)^{10} =$

    A. $-9$
    B. $-1$
    C. 0
    D. 1
    E. 9

Go, go, go to the next page.

*For problems 11 and 12:* Refer to the figure in the margin.

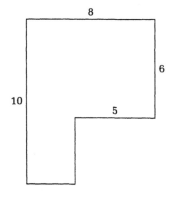

11.  The perimeter of the figure is

A.  29
B.  58
C.  36
D.  54
E.  72

12.  The area of this figure is

A.  80
B.  68
C.  60
D.  50
E.  40

*For problems 13 through 15:*  Refer to the figure below.

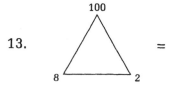

13.

A.  6⅔
B.  12
C.  16
D.  20
E.  25

14. 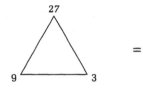    =

A.     B.     C.

D.     E.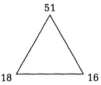

15.  If 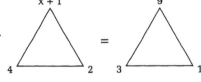 ,then x =

A.  1
B.  3
C.  5
D.  9
E.  impossible to tell

*For problems 16 and 17:* Given $y = \dfrac{x^2 - 8x + 12}{(x - 4)^2}$.

16.  If $y = 0$, then $x =$

A.  2, 6
B.  2, 4, 6
C.  −4, 2, 4, 6
D.  −4, 4
E.  4

Pretty please, go to the
next page.

17. For what value(s) of x does y have no value?

    A.  2, 6
    B.  2, 4, 6
    C.  −4, 2, 4, 6
    D.  −4, 4
    E.  4

18. Each brother has an equal number of sisters. Each sister has twice as many brothers. How many brothers and sisters are there?

    A.  2 brothers, 2 sisters
    B.  3 brothers, 3 sisters
    C.  3 brothers, 2 sisters
    D.  4 brothers, 3 sisters
    E.  6 brothers, 4 sisters

19. The volume of a cube is 64. Its surface area is

    A.  4
    B.  8
    C.  16
    D.  48
    E.  96

20. If this same cube has its faces colored, what is the minimum number of colors so that no 2 surfaces that touch have the same color?

    A.  1
    B.  2
    C.  3
    D.  4
    E.  5

21. The sum of measures of the angles of a triangle are consecutive integers. The largest is?

    A.  58
    B.  59
    C.  60
    D.  61
    E.  180

22. The fewest number of trees needed for 6 rows of 4 apple trees each is

    A. 24
    B. 23
    C. 20
    D. 19
    E. 12

23. An $875.20 TV is reduced in price by 50%. What % increase is needed to restore it to $875.20?

    A. 50%
    B. 75%
    C. 100%
    D. 150%
    E. 200%

24. The three semicircles are as pictured. Find their total area.

    A. $12.5\pi$
    B. $25\pi$
    C. $50\pi$
    D. $75\pi$
    E. $100\pi$

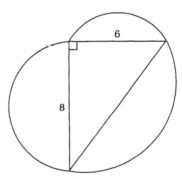

25. $2^n + 2^n =$

    A. $2^{n^2}$
    B. $2^{2n}$
    C. $4^{n^2}$
    D. $(2 + 2)^{n^2}$
    E. $2^{n+1}$

Stopppp nowwww!!

## PART 2

Solve the following problems and put the answers on your answer sheet. On the real SAT, you will fill in a gridddd.

25 questions, 35 minutes.

*For problems 1 through 3:* The number of people P in a city increases with the formula

$$P = 100,000 \times 4^{t/10}$$

t in years. It is 2060 now.

1. How many people now?

   A. 0
   B. 10
   C. 100,000
   D. 500,000
   E. 1,000,000

2. How many people will there be in the year 2080?

   A. 100,000
   B. 400,000
   C. 1,000,000
   D. 1,600,000
   E. 256,000,000

3. How many people will there be in the year 2065?

   A. 100,000
   B. 200,000
   C. 400,000
   D. 800,000
   E. 1,600,000

4. $2\begin{bmatrix} 4 & 0 \\ 0 & 5 \end{bmatrix} - \begin{bmatrix} 8 & 0 \\ 0 & 10 \end{bmatrix}$ is

   A. $\begin{bmatrix} 1 & 0 \\ 0 & 1 \end{bmatrix}$

B. $\begin{bmatrix} 0 & 0 \\ 0 & 0 \end{bmatrix}$

C. $\begin{bmatrix} 0 & 2 \\ 2 & 0 \end{bmatrix}$

D. $\begin{bmatrix} 0 & 0 \\ 0 & -10 \end{bmatrix}$

E. $\begin{bmatrix} 16 & 0 \\ 0 & -10 \end{bmatrix}$

5. $\begin{bmatrix} 3 & 0 \\ 0 & 4 \end{bmatrix} \times \begin{bmatrix} 0 & 1 \\ 1 & 0 \end{bmatrix}$ is

A. $\begin{bmatrix} 3 & 0 \\ 0 & 4 \end{bmatrix}$

B. $\begin{bmatrix} 0 & 3 \\ 4 & 0 \end{bmatrix}$

C. $\begin{bmatrix} 3 & 1 \\ 1 & 4 \end{bmatrix}$

D. $\begin{bmatrix} 0 & 0 \\ 0 & 0 \end{bmatrix}$

E. $\begin{bmatrix} 0 & 4 \\ 3 & 0 \end{bmatrix}$

6. $f(x) = x + 4^x.$    $f(1/2) + f(-1/2) =$

A. 5
B. 4 1/2
C. 2 1/2
D. 1
E. 0

7. $|x - 4| = |4 - x|. x =$

A. only 4
B. only −4
C. only 4 or −4

Go on to the next page;
yes, please do.

D. only 4, −4, 0

E. all values

8.   $b^{3/4} = 8$. b =

A. 6

B. 10 2/3

C. 16

D. 256/3

E. 256

9.   M is the midpoint of $\overline{AB}$, not pictured. A = (10, 3) and M = (5, 7). B =

A. (7.5, 5)

B. (0, 11)

C. (15, −1)

D. (50, 21)

E. $\sqrt{41}$

10.   $\overline{FG}$ is tangent to circle center O; F is the point of tangency.

Point H intersects $\overline{GO}$ on the circle. $\overline{OF} = 6$; $\overline{FG} = 8$. $\overline{HG} =$

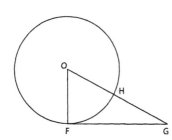

A. 2

B. 4

C. 6

D. 8

E. 10

11.   $-3 \le x \le 4 =$

A. $6 \le x^2 \le 8$

B. $9 \le x^2 \le 16$

C. $-9 \le x^2 \le 16$

D. $3 \le x^2 \le 4$

E. $0 \le x^2 \le 16$

*For problems 12 through 15*: Let (2, 4) be on the graph of f(x).

12.  On the graph f(x + 3), the point (2, 4) becomes

A. (5, 4)
B. (−1, 4)
C. (2, 1)
D. (2, 7)
E. (5, 7)

13.  On the graph f(x − 5), the point (2, 4) becomes

A. (7, 4)
B. (−3, 4)
C. (2, 9)
D. (2, −1)
E. (−3, −1)

14.  On the graph 2f(x), the point (2, 4) becomes

A. (4, 4)
B. (1, 4)
C. (2, 8)
D. (2, 2)
E. (4, 8)

15.  On the graph −2f(x − 3), the point (2, 4) becomes

A. (−10, −8)
B. (−10, 4)
C. (5, 4)
D. (5, 8)
E. (5, −8)

16.  How many rectangles 2 inches by 3 inches can be cut from a piece of paper that is 9 inches by 1 foot? 12 inches = 1 foot.

Go, go, go to the next page.

17. 15 less than 4 times a number is 5 more than twice the number. What is the number?

18. The perimeter of an equilateral triangle is exactly the same as the perimeter of an octagon. Find the ratio of the side of the triangle to the side of the octagon.

19. 8 people are standing in a circle. They shake each other's hands. How many handshakes are there if you count each pair shaking once and only once?

20. An octagon has how many diagonals?

21. A team has won 12 out of 20 games. How many games does the team have to win in a row for their winning percentage to be 75%?

22. If $1 < x < 50$, find the number of even numbers that are NOT multiples of 3.

23. Find the area.

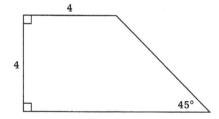

24. A rectangular box with a square base has a volume the same as a cylinder. One side of the base is $\sqrt{8\pi}$. The height of the box is 6. If the height of the cylinder is 3, find the radius of the base.

25. There are two numbers x such that the distance between (x, 3) and (2, 7) is 5. Find the sum of these numbers.

Stop!!!! This is the end of this section!!!!

## PART 3

Select your best choice, A, B, C, D, or E, and put it on your answer page. On the real SAT, you will fill in something.

10 questions, 15 minutes

1. J.D. wants to get an A in math. A 90 average is needed. J.D. has grades of 87, 79, and 96 on the first 3 tests. What does J.D. need for an A average?

   A. 88
   B. 92
   C. 96
   D. 98
   E. An A is not possible

2. After a 20% discount, a radio costs $56. What was the original cost?

   A. $44.80
   B. $67.20
   C. $70.00
   D. $76.00
   E. $80.00

3. At 10:25, a car left a location. 20 miles later at 10:40, the car arrived at its destination. The speed of the car was

   A. 40 mi/h
   B. 55 mi/h
   C. 60 mi/h
   D. 80 mi/h
   E. $132\frac{2}{3}$ mi/h

4. In 1996, U.S. Postal Service postage costs 32¢ for the first ounce and 23¢ for each additional ounce. Find the cost of mailing a ½-pound letter.

A. $1.93
B. $2.16
C. $2.17
D. $2.50
E. $2.52

5. △ABC and △BDQ are 2 ≅ isosceles right triangles. The coordinates of point Q are

A. (10, 0)
B. (10, −10)
C. (10, −20)
D. (20, −10)
E. (20, −20)

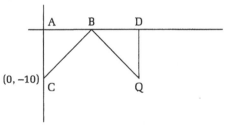

*For problems 6 through 10:* Each of the next five questions will have two statements, 1 and 2. Decide if each is true or false (if a statement is sometimes true, it is false):

Put A if 1 is false and 2 is false.

Put B if 1 is false and 2 is true.

Put C if 1 is true and 2 is false.

Put D if 1 is true and 2 is true, but they are not related.

Put E if 1 is true and 2 is true and they are related.

6.

1. If 2 parallel lines are cut by a transversal, the measure of all acute angles is congruent.

Go on to the next page.

   2. The sum of the measures of the angles of a polygon is 360°.

7.

   1. If $3x + 5 = 20$, then $x = 5$.

   2. If $2y + 7 = 15$, then $y = 4$.

8.

   1. The vertex angle of an isosceles triangle is 40°. One base angle is 70°.

   2. In a scalene triangle, either 2 angles may be equal or not.

9.

   1. The area of a rectangle is length times width.

   2. The area of a triangle is ½ base times height.

10.

   1. If you double the radius of a circle, you double its area.

Stop, stop, stop. I'm sure you want to. Let's check the answers.

   2. If you triple the edge of a cube, the volume increases by 6 times.

# ANSWER SHEET

| Part 1 | Part 2 | Part 3 |
| --- | --- | --- |
| 1. _____ | 1. _____ | 1. _____ |
| 2. _____ | 2. _____ | 2. _____ |
| 3. _____ | 3. _____ | 3. _____ |
| 4. _____ | 4. _____ | 4. _____ |
| 5. _____ | 5. _____ | 5. _____ |
| 6. _____ | 6. _____ | 6. _____ |
| 7. _____ | 7. _____ | 7. _____ |
| 8. _____ | 8. _____ | 8. _____ |
| 9. _____ | 9. _____ | 9. _____ |
| 10. _____ | 10. _____ | 10. _____ |
| 11. _____ | 11. _____ | |
| 12. _____ | 12. _____ | |
| 13. _____ | 13. _____ | |
| 14. _____ | 14. _____ | |
| 15. _____ | 15. _____ | |
| 16. _____ | 16. _____ | |
| 17. _____ | 17. _____ | |
| 18. _____ | 18. _____ | |
| 19. _____ | 19. _____ | |
| 20. _____ | 20. _____ | |
| 21. _____ | 21. _____ | |
| 22. _____ | 22. _____ | |
| 23. _____ | 23. _____ | |
| 24. _____ | 24. _____ | |
| 25. _____ | 25. _____ | |

## CHAPTER 24

# PRACTICE TEST II ANSWERS

## PART I

1. $3 - 5x$ is 6 less than $9 - 5x$. $5 - 6 = -1$.                  A

2. $2x + 5 + 65 = 180$. $2x = 110$. $x = 55$.                  C

3. Multiply by 12. $2x + x = 24$. $x = 8$.                  D

4. This is trial and error. $x = 8$, $y = 3$; $x + y = 11$.      B

5. Just count . . . 21, 28, 36, 45, 55.                  C

6. This is a real reading trick. You do not need
   the second equation at all. 2 bats plus 2 balls
   is $48. Soooooo, 1 of each is $24.                  C

7. $x^1 x^{a+b} x^{-b} = x^{a+1}$.                  D

8. When I did this the first time, my arithmetic wasn't too good. I hope yours is better.

   Subtracting, we get 2x + 2y = 28.

   Soooo                          x +  y = 14

   Annnnd                         $\dfrac{x + y}{2} = 7$                    A

9. $2^{60} = (2^3)^{4x}$. 12x = 60. x = 5.                    C

10. 1 − 1 + 1 − 1 + 1 − 1 + 1 − 1 + 1 = 0 + 0 + 0 + 0 + 1 = 1!                    D

*For Problems 11 and 12:*

   3 + 5 = 8

   6 + 4 = 10

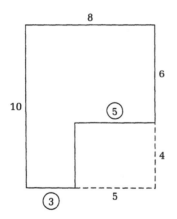

11. P = 10 + 8 + 6 + 4 + 5 + 3 = 36.                    C

12. A = 8 × 10 − 4 × 5 = 80 − 20 = 60.                    C

13. $\dfrac{100}{\dfrac{8}{2}} = \dfrac{100}{4} = 25$                    E

14. $\dfrac{27}{\dfrac{9}{3}} = \dfrac{27}{3} = 9$        $\dfrac{54}{\dfrac{12}{2}} = \dfrac{54}{6} = 9$                    B

15. $\dfrac{x + 1}{\dfrac{4}{2}} = \dfrac{9}{\dfrac{3}{1}}$        $\dfrac{x + 1}{2} = 3$      x + 1 = 6      x = 5   C

*For Problems 16 and 17:*

$$y = \frac{(x-6)(x-2)}{(x-4)(x-4)} \qquad y = 0 \qquad top = 0$$

No value bottom = 0

16.  x = 2, 6.                                                          A

17.  when x = 4, y has no value.                                       E

18.  Each brother has 3 brothers and 3 sisters.
     Each sister has 4 brothers and 2 sisters.                        D

19.  $e^3 = 64$. e = 4. $6e^2 = 6(16) = 96$.                          E

20.  
| | |
|---|---|
| 1 color | ABCD & EFGH |
| 1 color | BCGF & ADHE |
| 1 color | CDHG & ABFE |

The minimum number of colors is 3.                                    C

21.  x + x + 1 + x + 2 = 180. x = 59. x + 2 = 61.                     D

22.  Trick    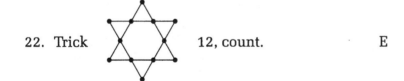    12, count.                      E

23.  Trick. The amount doesn't matter. $100 to $50.
     50% dip. $50 to $100. 100% increase.                            C

24.  The hypotenuse is 10, of course, thanks to old
     Pythag. A trick that would be nice to know to
     save time. We know $c^2 = a^2 + b^2$ (squares). It is
     also true for circles and semicircles. The two
     smaller semicircles add to the larger one. We only
     have to find the areas of the 2 largest semicircles,
     one full circle radius 5 (diameter is 10).                      B

25. We did this one. $2^n + 2^n = 1(2^n) + 1(2^n) = 2(2^n) = 2^1 2^n = 2^{n+1}$.                                E

# PART 2

1. If it is the year 2060, now means t = 0.
   $4^{0/10} = 1$; $1 \times 100{,}000 = 100{,}000$.                                              C

2. t = 2080 − 2060 = 20; $4^{20/10} = 4^2 = 16$; 16 ×
   100,000 = 1,600,000.                                                                           D

3. t = 2065 − 2060 = 5; $4^{5/10} = 4^{1/2} =$
   $\sqrt{4} = 2$; $2 \times 100{,}000 = 200{,}000$.                                              B

4. $\begin{bmatrix} 8 & 0 \\ 0 & 10 \end{bmatrix} - \begin{bmatrix} 8 & 0 \\ 0 & 10 \end{bmatrix} = B.$                 B

5. B.                                                                                             B

6. f(1/2) + f(−1/2) = 1/2 + $4^{1/2}$ + (−1/2) +
   $4^{-1/2}$ = 2 + 1/2 = 2 1/2                                                                   C

7. All real numbers.                                                                             E

8. b = $(b^{3/4})^{4/3} = 8^{4/3} = (\sqrt[3]{8})^4 = 2^4 = 16$.                                  C

9. A is (10, 3), and M is (5, 7). The x values
   go down 5; they go up 4. The answer is B.                                                     B

10. $\overline{GO} = 10$. We have a 6-8-10 right triangle, since
    the radius is perpendicular to a tangent at the
    point of tangency:

    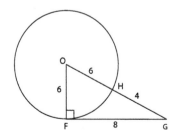

    $\overline{OH}$, a radius = 6. $\overline{GO} - \overline{HO} = \overline{GH} = 4$.          B

11. Tricky!!! The answer is E. Look closely.                                                     E

12. f(x + 3) is 3 to the left.                                                                   B

13. f(x − 5) is 5 to the right.                                                                  A

14. 2 f(x) means the y value is multiplied by 2.     C

15. $-2f(x - 3)$: $x - 3$: 3 to the right; $-2$: Then the
   y is twice as big buuut upside down ($-y$).     E

16. $2 \times 3 = 6$     $9 \times 12 = 108$     $108 \div 6 = 18$

17. $4n - 15 = 2n + 5$
   $\phantom{4n - 15} 2n = 20$
   $\phantom{4n - 15aa} n = 10$

18. $3s = 8\theta$     $s/\theta = 8/3$

19. Each person shakes 7 hands, but each is
   counted twice. Sooooo $(8)(7)/2 = 28$.

20. Looks the same but isn't. Each vertex can't be
   drawn to itself or to either side. 5 total are left.
   Each is counted twice. $5(8)/2 = 20$. There is a
   formula if you like. The number of diagonals
   is $n(n - 3)/2$. $n \geq 3$.

21. $\dfrac{12 + x}{20 + x} = \dfrac{3}{4}$ (75%)     $4x + 48 = 3x + 60$     $x = 12$

22. 2 into 48 is 24. 6 into 48 is 8 (mult of 6 are
   both 2 and 3). $24 - 8 = 16$.

23. Area = trapezoid or square + triangle =
   $16 + 8 = 24$.

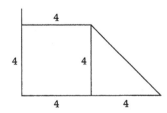

24. $V = s \times s \times h = \sqrt{8\pi} \times \sqrt{8\pi} \times 6 = 48\pi$. $V = \pi r^2 h = 48\pi$. $h = 3$. $\pi r^2 = 16\pi$. $r^2 = 16$. $r = 4$.

25. $(x - 2)^2 + (7 - 3)^2 = 25.$ $x^2 - 4x + 4 + 16 = 25.$
    $x^2 - 4x - 5 = 0.$ $(x - 5)(x + 1) = 0.$ $x = 5.$
    $x = -1.$   $5 + -1 = 4.$

# PART 3

1. $87 + 79 + 96 = 262.$ $90 \times 4 = 360.$ $360 - 262 =$
   98. Tough A, but possible.                           D

2. You've got to know percents: $.8x = 56.$ $x =$
   $\$70 = \dfrac{560}{8}.$                               C

3. 15 minutes. 1 little quarter of an hour.
   $4 \times 20 = 80$ mi/h.                               D

4. 32¢ + 7 (not 8) × 23¢ = $1.93.                        A

5.                                                        D

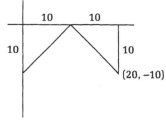

6. 1 is true. 2 is false (should be quadrilateral).      C

7. Both are true, but certainly unrelated.               D

8.

   1. $40 + 2x = 180.$ $2x = 140.$ $x = 70.$ True.

2. Scalene all sides not equal means all angles not equal. False.            C

9. A triangle is 1/2 a rectangle. I hope you've been told that. Both true and related.         E

10. $r = 10\pi$. $A = 100\pi$. $r = 20$. $A = 400\pi$. False (4 times; not 2). $e = 2$. $e^3 = 8$. $e = 6$. $e^3 = 216$. $216/8 = 27$ times, not 6. False.         A

Let's take a deep breath and try one more test.

# PRACTICE TEST III

## PART I

Select the best answer A, B, C, D, or E to each question, and write its letter on the answer sheet at the end of this chapter.

25 questions, 30 minutes

1. We say A is a subset of B if every element in A is also in B. B = {d, e, f} has how many 1- or 2-element subsets?

   A. 6
   B. 7
   C. 8
   D. 9
   E. more than 9

2. $f(x) = \dfrac{x^2 - 2x - 3}{x - 4}$ is not defined if x =

   A.  4
   B.  3, −1
   C.  4, 3, −1
   D.  1
   E.  0

Go, go, go on to the next page.

3. $|x| = -x$ if $x$ is

   A. only 0
   B. only 0 and 1
   C. only 0 and −1
   D. only nonpositive integers
   E. only nonpositive real numbers

4. The radius of a cylinder is multiplied by 5; the height is multiplied by 4. The volume is multiplied by

   A. 4
   B. 5
   C. 20
   D. 100
   E. 400

5. If $p = 1/q$, then $\dfrac{1 - \dfrac{1}{q}}{\dfrac{1}{p} - 1} =$

   A. −1
   B. 1
   C. p
   D. −p
   E. −p²

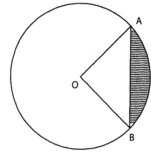

6. A circle, center O, has a section with equilateral triangle OAB. $\overline{AB} = 6$. The area of the shaded portion is

   A. $9(4\pi - \sqrt{3})$
   B. $36(\pi - 3)$
   C. $6(\pi - 6\sqrt{3})$
   D. $3(2\pi - 3\sqrt{3})$
   E. $6(\pi - 3)$

7. 456, written as powers of 10, is $4 \times 10^2 + 5 \times 10^1 + 6$. If 194, presently in powers of 10, were written as powers of 5, the number would be

A. 1234
B. 4321
C. 1324
D. 2413
E. 4132

8. 456, written as powers of 10, is $4 \times 10^2 + 5 \times 10^1 + 6$. On a computer, everything is written in powers of 2 using only zeros and ones. As written, 10011 is in powers of 2. In powers of 10, the number would be

A. 38
B. 19
C. 14
D. 7
E. 3

9. If $x = 4$, then $x^{1/2} + x^{-1/2} + x^2 + x^{-2} =$

A. 0
B. 4
C. 12 5/8
D. 18 9/16
E. more than 30

10. Given point A (0, 0), point B (0, 8), and point C (−6, 0). The distance between the midpoint of $\overline{AB}$ and the midpoint of $\overline{AC}$ is

A. 3
B. 4
C. 5
D. 10
E. (−1.5, 2)

11. $\sqrt{x - 1} = x - 1$ is true for what values of x?

A. only 1
B. only 1 and 2

Go, go, go on to the next page.

C. only 0, 1, and 2
D. only −1, 0, 1
E. all real numbers

12. $f(x) = f(-x)$. If $f(a) = 4$, then $f(-a) =$

A. −4
B. −2
C. 0
D. 2
E. 4

13. $\dfrac{x}{a} + \dfrac{x}{b} = 1$. $(a + b) x =$

A. a
B. b
C. a + b
D. ab
E. $\dfrac{1}{a} + \dfrac{1}{b}$

14. The solution to $|x - 3| < -1$ is

A. $2 < x < 4$
B. $x > 4$ or $x < 2$
C. $x < 2$
D. all real numbers
E. no real numbers

15. $f(x) = x + 4^x$, and $g(x) = x + 2^{4x+6}$. $f(x) = g(x)$ if $x =$

A. −6
B. −3
C. 0
D. 3
E. 6

16. $\dfrac{(9 - x)^2}{2} = \dfrac{(x - 3)^2}{2}$     $x =$

A. 0
B. 3
C. 4
D. 6
E. 8

17. $\left(\dfrac{a^4 b^7}{a^6 b^4}\right)^3 =$

   A. $\dfrac{b^9}{a^6}$

   B. $\dfrac{b^{281}}{a^{256}}$

   C. $\dfrac{b^3}{a^2}$

   D. $a^6 b^{17}$

   E. $a^{58} b^{339}$

18. $\left(\dfrac{6 \times 6 \times 6}{6 + 6 + 6}\right) y = 6. \ y =$

   A. 1/6
   B. 1/2
   C. 6
   D. 36
   E. 216

19. $\dfrac{80 + 2x}{8}$ is equivalent to

   A. $10 + 2x$
   B. $80 + x/4$
   C. $(80 + x)/4$
   D. $(10 + x)/4$
   E. $10 + \dfrac{x}{4}$

Go rapidly to the next page.

20. $\dfrac{x^2 + 9x + 8}{x^2 + 4x + 4} = 1.$ $x =$

    A. $-17/8$
    B. $-4/5$
    C. $-2$
    D. $-1$
    E. $-8$

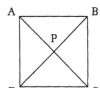

21. ABCD is a square. $\overline{BP} = 6$. The area is

    A. $144$
    B. $72\sqrt{2}$
    C. $72$
    D. $36\sqrt{2}$
    E. $36$

22. Speaking of squares, if you add 3 inches to the length and subtract 3 inches from the width, the area of the new rectangle is

    A. 9 square inches less than the square.
    B. 3 square inches less than the square.
    C. the same as the square.
    D. 3 square inches more than the square.
    E. 9 square inches more than the square.

23. $\left(x - \dfrac{1}{x}\right)^2 = 100$      $x^2 + \dfrac{1}{x^2} =$

    A. $8$
    B. $12$
    C. $98$
    D. $102$
    E. $10,000$

24. Which letter indicates a 50% increase from 1 to 2
    followed by a 50% decrease from 2 to 3?

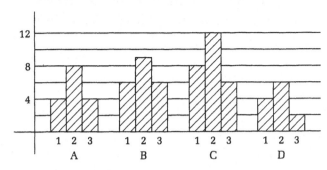

   A. A
   B. B
   C. C
   D. D
   E. none of these

25. A clock rings at equal intervals forever: ding,
    ding, ding, ding, ding, . . . The bell rings 6 times
    in 5 seconds. In 30 seconds the bell rings how
    many times?

   A. 30
   B. 31
   C. 36
   D. 40
   E. 61

It is time to stop for a
moment. STOP!!!!

## PART 2

Select the correct answer and fill it in on the answer sheet at the end of the chapter. The SAT does it differently.

25 questions, 25 minutes

1.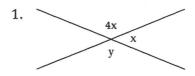

   $y =$

   A. 18
   B. 36
   C. 72
   D. 108
   E. 144

2. $x^4 - 17 = 64.$ $x^4 =$

   A. 81
   B. 9
   C. $\pm 9$
   D. 3
   E. $\pm 3$

3. $(10ab^2)^3 =$

   A. $30ab^5$
   B. $30ab^6$
   C. $1000ab^6$
   D. $1000a^3b^5$
   E. $1000a^3b^6$

4. 4 zoups = 7 zims annnnd 8 zims = 11 zounds. The ratio of zoups/zounds is

A. 77/32
B. 32/77
C. 7/22
D. 22/7
E. 2

5. The value of q quarters and d dimes is

A. d + q
B. 10d + q
C. 10(d + 25q)
D. 25(d + q)
E. 10d + 25q

6.

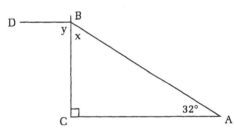

(figure not drawn to scale)

$\overline{AC}$ is parallel to $\overline{BD}$. x + y =

A. 90
B. 122
C. 132
D. 138
E. 148

7. $\dfrac{\dfrac{3}{4}}{3m} =$

Let's journey to the next page.

A. m/4
B. 4/m
C. 36/m
D. m/36
E. 9m/4

8. If $x = 10$, then $(10x)^2 + 10x^2 =$

A. 10,100
B. 11,000
C. 20,000
D. 100,000
E. 10,000,000

*For Problems 9 and 10:*
$a * b = 2ab + b.$

9. $4 * 5 =$

A. 44
B. 45
C. 160
D. 200
E. 9

10. If $a * b = 0$ and $b \neq 0$, then $a =$

A. $-1/4$
B. $-1/2$
C. 0
D. 1
E. 2

11. The equation that best illustrates the chart is

A. $y = 2x^2 - 4$
B. $y = x^2$
C. $y = 3x - 2$
D. $y = x + 3$
E. $y = 2x - 1$

| x | 1 | 2 | 3 | 4 |
|---|---|---|---|---|
| y | 1 | 4 | 7 | 10 |

12. k/2 odd and k/5 even. k could be

A. 15
B. 20
C. 30
D. 40
E. 60

13. $x = \dfrac{ay}{b} + c$. Then y =

A. abc + c
B. (bx − c)/a
C. (bx + c)/a
D. (ab − ac)/x
E. (bx − bc)/a

14. O is the center of the circle. $\overline{OB} = 5$, and BC = 2. The area of the shaded region is

A. 75π
B. 21π
C. 24π
D. 74π
E. 32π

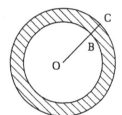

15. O is the center of the circle. The radius is 10. The area of the shaded part is

A. 25(π − 1)
B. 25(π − 2)
C. 100(π − 1/4)
D. 50(π − 1)
E. 50(π − 2)

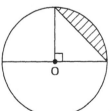

16. For the line 4x + 5y = 20, the slope is

A. 20
B. −5
C. −4
D. −4/5
E. −5/4

Please continue to next page.

17. $10^2 - (-8)^2 =$

    A.  36
    B.  −36
    C.  164
    D.  6400
    E.  4

18. The ratio of angle A to angle B is 3:2. Angle A =

    A.  30
    B.  60
    C.  75
    D.  90
    E.  120

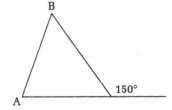

(figure not drawn to scale)

19. If $y = x^2/z^3$, then $xy/z =$

    A.  $x^3/z^4$
    B.  $x/z^2$
    C.  $x^3/z^3$
    D.  $x/z$
    E.  $xz$

20. $9^{3x+3} = 27^{4x-5}$      $x =$

    A.  8
    B.  5
    C.  7/2
    D.  5/2
    E.  3

21. A basketball team has 4 players whose heights are 6 feet 7 inches, 6 feet 9 inches, 6 feet 10 inches, and 7 feet 1 inch. How tall must the 5th player be so the average (arithmetic mean) is 7 feet?

A. 7 feet 3 inches
B. 7 feet 6 inches
C. 7 feet 9 inches
D. 7 feet 11 inches
E. 8 feet

22. ABCD is a square. $\overline{AB} = 1$. The area of the entire region is

A. $1 + \pi$
B. $1 + \pi/2$
C. $1 + \pi/4$
D. $4 + \pi$
E. $4 + \pi/2$

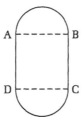

23. O is the center of the circle. $\overline{CO} = 6$. The area of the shaded part $= 24\pi$. $\measuredangle x =$

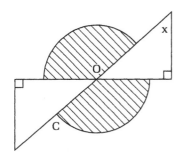

A. 15°
B. 30°
C. 45°
D. 60°
E. 100°

24. $x =$

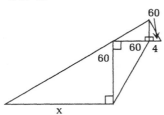

Shhhh. Quietly but quickly go on to the next page.

A. 9
B. $9\sqrt{3}$
C. 16
D. $16\sqrt{3}$
E. 36

25.

| year 5770 | year 6000 |
|-----------|-----------|
| 32,000 glzrs | 80,000 glzrs |

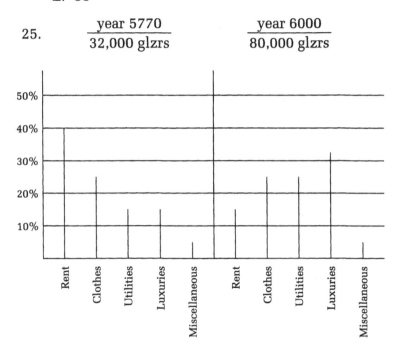

On planet zyzxz, in the year 5770, the budget was 32,000 glzrs. In the year 6000, the budget was 80,000 glzrs. Which part of the budget, approximately, was the same number of glzrs?

A. rent
B. clothes
C. utilities
D. luxuries
E. miscellaneous

Stopppp!!!!

# PART 3

Find the answer to each question, and put its letter on the answer sheet at the end of chapter. The SAT will have you fill in a silly grid.

10 questions, 15 minutes

1. Find the sum of all the primes between 50 and 60.

2. The product of two consecutive even positive integers is 48. The quotient of the larger divided by the smaller is what?

3. Find a fraction between 7/8 and 7/9. There may be no decimal in the answer, and the denominator must be less than 100.

4. The sum of 15 consecutive integers is 0. Find the product of the two smallest.

5. $4^{n+1} = 64$. $2^{n+2} + 3^{n+1} + 5^{n-1} =$

6.

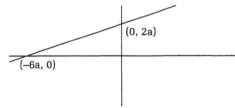

(0, 2a)

(−6a, 0)

The slope of this line is what?

7. The supplement of an angle is 6 times the complement. Find the angle.

8. The surface area of a cube is the same as the numerical volume of that cube. The edge of the cube is what?

9. 9.1235781235781. . . . After the decimal point, the 89th digit is what?

10. How many $7 tickets must be sold with $4 tickets so that the average of 24 tickets is $6?

Stop, oh please stop, and let's check the answers since it is the end of the test.

# ANSWER SHEET

| Part 1 | Part 2 | Part 3 |
|--------|--------|--------|
| 1. _____ | 1. _____ | 1. _____ |
| 2. _____ | 2. _____ | 2. _____ |
| 3. _____ | 3. _____ | 3. _____ |
| 4. _____ | 4. _____ | 4. _____ |
| 5. _____ | 5. _____ | 5. _____ |
| 6. _____ | 6. _____ | 6. _____ |
| 7. _____ | 7. _____ | 7. _____ |
| 8. _____ | 8. _____ | 8. _____ |
| 9. _____ | 9. _____ | 9. _____ |
| 10. _____ | 10. _____ | 10. _____ |
| 11. _____ | 11. _____ | |
| 12. _____ | 12. _____ | |
| 13. _____ | 13. _____ | |
| 14. _____ | 14. _____ | |
| 15. _____ | 15. _____ | |
| 16. _____ | 16. _____ | |
| 17. _____ | 17. _____ | |
| 18. _____ | 18. _____ | |
| 19. _____ | 19. _____ | |
| 20. _____ | 20. _____ | |
| 21. _____ | 21. _____ | |
| 22. _____ | 22. _____ | |
| 23. _____ | 23. _____ | |
| 24. _____ | 24. _____ | |
| 25. _____ | 25. _____ | |

## CHAPTER 26

# PRACTICE TEST III
# ANSWERS

## PART I

1. The answer is 6, A. The sets are {1}, {2}, {3}, {1, 2}, {1, 3}, and {2, 3}. Order doesn't matter, and repeated elements don't count!     A

2. The only bad number(s) is (are) where the bottom equals 0. The answer is A.     A

3. The answer is E. (See it by substitution.)     E

4. If we originally let r = 1 and h = 1, the volume is π. If we let r = 5 and h = 4, the new volume is $\pi r^2 h = \pi(5^2)(4) = 100\,\pi$, one hundred times the original.     D

5. Substituting, multiplying the top and bottom by p and NOT multiplying out the top, we get

$$\frac{(1-p)p}{\left(1-\dfrac{1}{p}\right)p} = \frac{(1-p)p}{(p-1)} = -1(p) = -p$$ The answer

is D.     D

6. Area $= \dfrac{1}{6}\pi r^2 - \dfrac{s^2 \sqrt{3}}{4} = \dfrac{1}{6}\pi(6)^2 - \dfrac{6^2 \sqrt{3}}{4} =$

   $6\pi - 9\sqrt{3} = 3(2\pi - 3\sqrt{3}).$                                                 D

7. When a similar question appeared on the SAT, I thought this was totally unfair. The way to do this is to divide repeatedly by 5. The answer is the remainders in the reverse order. 194/5 = 38R4. 38/5 = 7R3. 7/5 = 1R2. 1/5 = 0R1. Answer? 1234.

   To check: $1 \times 5^3 + 2 \times 5^2 + 3 \times 5 + 4 =$
   $125 + 50 + 15 + 4 = 194.$                                                              A

8. Based on problem 7, 10011 $= 1 \times 2^4 + 0 \times 2^3 + 0 \times 2^2 + 1 \times 2 + 1 = 19.$                B

9. $4^{1/2} + 4^{-1/2} + 4^2 + 4^{-2} = 2 + \dfrac{1}{2} + 16 + \dfrac{1}{16} = 18\,\dfrac{9}{16}.$                D

10. The midpoint of $\overline{AB} = (0, 4)$. The midpoint of $\overline{AC} = (-3, 0)$. The distance between these points is $\sqrt{(-3-0)^2 + (4-0)^2} = 5.$ CCCC.              C

11. Substitution is the easiest way. The answer is B.                                        B

12. The answer is E, 4.                                                                      E

13. Multiply both sides by ab, the LCD. The answer is D.                                      D

14. The absolute value can't ever be negative and can't be less than a negative number. The answer is E.                                                                      E

15. $x + 4^x = x + 2^{4x+6}$; $4^x = 2^{4x+6}$; $(2)^{2x} = 2^{4x+6}$;

$2x = 4x + 6; x = -3.$         B

16. Hopefully by looking, you can see that if you substitute $x = 6$, the two sides are equal. The 2s at the bottom are there to throw you: $[3^2 = (-3)^2]$.     D

17. Almost all the time it is better to simplify the inside of the parentheses first. When you divide, you subtract exponents

$$\left(\frac{b^3}{a^2}\right)^3 = \frac{b^9}{a^6}$$

because a power to a power means to multiply exponents.     A

18. The easiest way, I think . . .

$$\frac{6 \times 6 \times 6}{18} \, y$$

Now cancel:

$$\frac{\overset{1}{\cancel{6}} \times \overset{2}{\cancel{6}} \times 6}{\underset{3}{\cancel{18}} \quad 1} \, y = 12y = 6$$

Soooo, $y = 6/12 = 1/2$.     B

Hopefully you did it a lot faster than it took me to type it.

19. Split it: $\dfrac{80 + 2x}{8} = \dfrac{80}{8} + \dfrac{2x}{8} = 10 + \dfrac{x}{4}$.     E

20. Cross multiply: $\dfrac{x^2 + 9x + 8}{x^2 + 4x + 4} = \dfrac{1}{1}$.

$x^2 + 9x + 8 = x^2 + 4x + 4$. Cancel the $x^2$'s.

$9x + 8 = 4x + 4.\ 5x = -4.\ x = -4/5.$                                B

21. There are several ways to do this, but here are two:

    a. $\overline{PB} = 6.$ $\overline{BC} = 6\sqrt{2}$, a 45-45-90 triangle.
       $A = (6\sqrt{2})^2 = 72.$

    b. $\overline{PC}$ is also 6. The area of triangle BPC is
       $\frac{1}{2}6 \times 6 = 18.$

    There are 4 triangles: $4 \times 18 = 72$. There are other ways, but all of them better give the same answer. Otherwise, there is no mathematics.                C

22. Take any number, say, 5. $5^2 = 25$. Then
    $(5 + 3)(5 - 3) = 16$. $16 - 25 = -9$. Orrrr
    $(x - 3)(x + 3) - x^2 = x^2 - 9 - x^2 = -9.$
    The answer is still A.                                A

23. This is a toughie because there are several things you could do, but the correct one is to just multiply it out:

    $$\left(x - \frac{1}{x}\right)^2 = \left(x - \frac{1}{x}\right)\left(x - \frac{1}{x}\right) = x^2 - 2(x)\left(\frac{1}{x}\right) + \frac{1}{x^2}$$

    $$= x^2 + \frac{1}{x^2} - 2 = 100$$

    Sooooo, $x^2 + \frac{1}{x^2} = 100 + 2 = 102.$                D

24. A: 4 to 8 is a 100% increase. A is wrong.

    B: 6 to 9 is a 50% increase. 3/6 (try to leave these as fractions when you do these problems). Buuut 9 to 6 is −3/9, which is not a

50% increase. B is wrong.

C: 8 to 12 is a 50% increase. 4/8. 12 to 6 is a
50% decrease. 6/12. The answer is C.          C

25. This is not, not, not a ratio portion. The question
is how long between dings? When you count, you
start after the first ring. If a bell rings 6 times in

| 1 sec | 1 sec | 1 sec | 1 sec | 1 sec |
|---|---|---|---|---|
| 1 | 2 | 3 | 4 | 5 | 6 rings |

5 seconds, there is 1 second between rings. See
the picture. So in 30 seconds, the bell rings 30
times + 1 at the beginning, 31.          B

# PART 2

1. $4x + x = 180$. $5x = 180$. $x = 36$. $4x = 4(36) =$
$144 = y$.          E

2. Remember, you are solving for $x^4$. Don't do
toooo much. $x^4 = 64 + 17 = 81$. That's it!          A

3. $(10ab^2)(10ab^2)(10ab^2) = 1000a^3b^6$.          E

4. $\dfrac{4 \text{ zoups}}{11 \text{ zounds}} = \dfrac{7 \text{ zims}}{8 \text{ zims}}$     zims cancel

$\dfrac{4 \text{ zoups}}{11 \text{ zounds}} = \dfrac{7}{8}$

Multiply both sides by 11/4:

$\dfrac{\text{Zoups}}{\text{Zounds}} = \dfrac{7}{8} \times \dfrac{11}{4} = \dfrac{77}{32}$          A

5. Quarters are 25¢. Dimes are 10¢. The total

value is 10d + 25q.                                                    E

6. x is the complement of 32. x = 58. 58 +
   90 = 148.                                                           E

7. 3 divided by 4/3m. Flip 4/3m upside down
   and multiply:

   $$\frac{3}{1} \times \frac{3m}{4} = \frac{9m}{4}$$                  E

8. $(10 \times 10)^2 + 10(10)^2 = 10,000 + 1,000 = 11,000.$    B

*For problems 9 and 10:*  a * b = 2ab + b.

9. $4 * 5 = 2(4)(5) + 5 = 40 + 5 = 45.$                               B

10. $2ab + b = 0.$ $2ab = -b.$ $a = -b/2b = -\frac{1}{2}.$             B

11. You must substitute at least 3 numbers to be
    sure, unless you know that the chart is the
    equation of a line. Then only 2 numbers are
    needed. The answer is y = 3x − 2:
    y = 3(1) − 2 = 1; y = 3(2) − 2 = 4
    y = 3(3) − 2 = 7                                                   C

12. By trial and error, k = 30. 30/2 is odd and
    30/5 is even.                                                     C

13.        $x = \dfrac{ay}{b} + c$       Multiply by b.

           $bx = ay + bc$       Subtract bc.

           $bx - bc = ay$           Divide by a.

           $\dfrac{bx - bc}{a} = y$                                    E

Remember, if you are terrible at problems like this,

don't worry. If there are 8 problems you absolutely can't do, getting the other 52 right means 700 plus. You must concentrate on getting right what you know.

14. The area of a "ring" is the area of the outer circle minus the area of the inner:

$r_{out} = 5 + 2 = 7$    $r_{in} = 5$.    $49\pi - 25\pi = 24\pi$        C

15. Normally on a real SAT, there would not be two questions involving the area of a circle. But this is practice. The shaded portion issss the area of ¼ of a circle minus the area of a triangle:

$A = \frac{1}{4}\pi 10^2 - \frac{1}{2}(10)(10) = 25\pi - 50 = 25(\pi - 2)$        B

16. You can substitute points, but the easiest way is to solve for x and the coefficient of x is the slope:

$4x + 5y = 20$        $5y = -4x + 20$

$\dfrac{5y}{5} = \dfrac{-4x}{5} + \dfrac{20}{5}$        $-4/5$        D

17. $10^2 - (-8)(-8) = 100 - 64 = 36$.        A

18. The exterior angle is the sum of the remote interior angles. Angle A plus angle B = 150:

$3x + 2x = 150$    $5x = 150$        $x = 30$    $3x = 90$    D

19. $y = \dfrac{x^2}{z^3}$        $\dfrac{xy}{z} = \dfrac{x^2(x)}{z^3(z)} = \dfrac{x^3}{z^4}$        A

20. $9^{3x+3} = 27^{4x-5}$.        We must see that 9 and 27 are powers of 3. $9 = 3^2$. $27 = 3^3$.

$(3^2)^{3x+3} = (3^3)^{4x-5}$.        If the bases are the same, the exponents must be the same:

$$2(3x + 3) = 3(4x - 5)$$

$$6x + 6 = 12x - 15$$

$$-6x = -21$$

$$x = -21/-6 = 7/2 \qquad\qquad\qquad C$$

21. This is an averaging problem, but if you add up all the heights, you may take forever. The average must be 7 feet:

6 feet 7 inches = −5 inches from 7 feet

6 feet 9 inches = −3 inches

6 feet 10 inches = −2 inches

7 feet 1 inch = +1 inch      The total is −9 inches.
So the center (the 5th player) must be
7 feet 9 inches, BIG!!! $\qquad\qquad\qquad$ C

22.

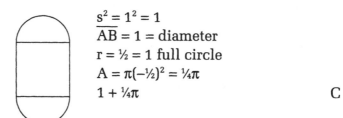

$$s^2 = 1^2 = 1$$
$$\overline{AB} = 1 = \text{diameter}$$
$$r = \tfrac{1}{2} = 1 \text{ full circle}$$
$$A = \pi(-\tfrac{1}{2})^2 = \tfrac{1}{4}\pi$$
$$1 + \tfrac{1}{4}\pi \qquad\qquad\qquad C$$

23. The area of the circle $= \pi(6)^2 = 36\pi$.

$$\frac{24\pi}{36\pi} = \frac{2}{3} \text{ of } \odot$$

2 vertical ∡s at 0      1/3 of ⊙
⅓(360) = 120°

1 angle at 0 = ½(120) = 60
x = 90 − 60 = 30 $\qquad\qquad\qquad$ B

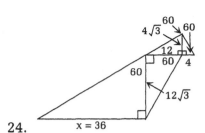

24. x = 36           E

25. Forget about the last 3 zeros (32,~~000~~, 80,~~000~~):

.40(32) = 12.8      .15(80) = 12       A

The rest are totally different.

# PART 3

1. After 2, all primes are odd. 51 is divisible by 3, as is 57. 55 is divisible by 5. 53 + 59 = 112.

2. Trial and error: $6 \times 8 = 48$. $8/6 = 4/3$.

3. $\dfrac{7}{9} = \dfrac{56}{72}$      $\dfrac{7}{8} = \dfrac{63}{72}$

   57/72, 58/72, 59/72, 60/72, 61/72, and 62/72 are all OK.

4. $-7 + -6 + -5 + -4 + -3 + -2 + -1 + 0 + 1 + 2 + 3 + 4 + 5 + 6 + 7$

   $(-7)(-6) = 42$

5. $4^{7+1} = 4^3 = 64$    $n + 1 = 3$    $n = 2$    $2^{2+2} + 3^{2+1} + 5^{2-1} = 16 + 27 + 5 = 48$

6. $m = \dfrac{2a - 0}{0 - (-6a)} = \dfrac{2a}{6a} = \dfrac{1}{3}$

7. A toughie. x = angle. 180 − x = supplement of x. 90 − x = complement of x:

$$180 - x = 6(90 - x)$$

$$180 - x = 540 - 6x$$

$$5x = 360$$

$$x = 72$$

8.  $x^3 = 6x^2$. $x = 6$.

9.  Don't look at 9. Repeats every 6 places. $6\overline{)89}$ $\overset{14R5}{}$ . Fifth place is 7.

10. Story and word problem. But, again, worry only about what you don't know. This really isn't too bad:

| Cost/Ticket | ×Tickets | = $ |
|---|---|---|
| $7 | x | = 7x |
| 4 | 24 − x | = 4(24 − x) |
| 6 | 24 | = 144 |

**Trial and error might work if you have the time.**

$$7x + 4(24 - x) = 144$$

$$3x + 96 = 144$$

$$3x = 48$$

$$x = 16$$

# HOW TO TAKE THE REAL SAT

You might ask, "Now that I've finished your book, what should I do?" If I were you, this is what I'd do.

1. Buy the ETS book *10 Real SATs*. These are real SATs to practice, which you want to do. There is extra stuff in the book that might help you too, but practicing real SATs is important. Practice them for time also.

2. Study as much as you want until two days before the SAT. Say your SAT is on a Wednesday, which it probably won't be. The last time I would study heavily would be Monday afternoon. After that, relax. I believe that your subconscious has answers. If you are relaxed, your subconscious may give you 50 or more points.

3. If you must study a little the last two days, only study a couple of problems, a couple of formulas, or a couple of words that will bother you if you don't know them. Last-minute cramming on this test does not help.

4. The night before, have everything ready to go for the morning: test forms, entrance cards, ID, pencils, calculator (for security), and anything else you might need.

5. Go to sleep at the same time you normally do for school (unless you don't get enough sleep nor-

mally). If you go to bed too late or too early, you probably will not be rested properly.

6. In the morning eat breakfast, even if you do not normally eat breakfast. Experiments have shown students that eat, perform better.

7. Dress comfortably.

8. If you are a slow starter—that is, it takes you a couple of minutes to get up to full speed—start out with two easy math problems and two easy English problems at home before you go to the test. Because all the tests are timed, you must be going at full blast almost immediately. The problems you start with should be easy so that you won't kill your confidence.

9. Bring some food and/or drinks with you to keep up your energy level.

10. Arrive at the room early. This will make you more relaxed.

11. It is OK to be a little nervous. Once the test starts, you should be fine. The SAT is the one test in all of high school I wasn't nervous for. For regular high school tests, I would say to myself, "Did I study enough? Did I study the right thing?" However, no matter how much you study, the SAT can always put in something you've never seen. You'll probably miss it. There is nothing you can do. Just concentrate on getting what you know correct.

12. Guess if you don't know. If you are average, you will break even. If you are unlucky, you may lose a few more points. If you are lucky or you can eliminate one or more of the multiple-choice answers, you may get a lot of extra points!!!!

13. Never spend too much time on one question.

14. Use your calculator as little as possible.

15. Never change an answer unless you are 100% sure. First answers are almost always best. Annnd

16. Have fun!!!!

GOOD LUCK!!!!GOOD LUCK!!!!GOOD LUCK!!!!GOOD LUCK!!!!
GOOD LUCK!!!!

# ABOUT BOB MILLER...
# IN HIS OWN WORDS

After attending George W. Hewlett High School in Hewlett, Long Island, New York, I received my BS and MS in math from Polytechnic University. After the first class that I taught as a substitute for a full professor, one student told another upon leaving the room that "at least we have someone that can teach the stuff."

From then on, I was forever hooked on teaching. I have taught more than 30 years in college math departments: CUNY, Rutgers, Westfield State, and Poly. I am in the seventh and eighth editions of *Who's Who Among American Teachers*. My main blessing is my large and expanding family: wife Marlene, daughter Sheryl, son Eric, son-in-law Glenn, daughter-in-law Wanda, and four wonderful grandchildren: Kira, Evan, Sean, and Sarah. My hobbies are golf, bowling, and crossword puzzles.

To me, teaching math is always a great joy. I hope I can give some of the joy to you.

# NOTES

# NOTES